# HISTORIC PUBS
# OF DUBLIN

AUBREY MALONE grew up in the west of Ireland and moved to Dublin in 1969. A full-time writer and journalist, his many books include fiction and biography and lighter works such as *The Sayings of Brendan Behan* and *The Guinness Book of Humorous Irish Anecdotes*. He has been a barman in both London and New York but his apprenticeship in Dublin's pubs has been spent on the other side of the counter.

# HISTORIC PUBS OF DUBLIN

AUBREY MALONE

PHOTOGRAPHY BY TREVOR HART

**NEW
ISLAND**

Published in 2001 in Ireland by
New Island Books, 2 Brookside, Dundrum Road, Dublin 14

First published in Great Britain by Prion Books Limited
Text copyright © Aubrey Malone 2001
Design and photography copyright © Prion Books 2001
Photography by Trevor Hart

A catalogue record for this book is available from the British Library.

ISBN  I 902602 49 8

Cover design by Bob Eames
Designed by DW Design, London. www.dwdesign.co.uk
Colour reproduction by Omnia Scanners, Milan, Italy
Printed in China by Everbest

# Contents

INTRODUCTION............................10

## The City Centre

The Lord Edward................................22

The Castle Inn.........................................25

Mother Red Caps................................29

The Brazen Head.................................33

The Long Hall.......................................38

The Stag's Head ..................................43

The Old Stand.....................................45

Grogan's ..................................................48

The International ..............................51

O'Neill's..................................................54

Bowe's ......................................................58

The Long Stone ..................................60

Mulligan's ..............................................63

The Oval ..................................................68

The Flowing Tide.............................72

The Parnell Mooney .........................75

Patrick Conway's...................................78

Nancy Hand's.........................................80

Ryan's of Parkgate Street ..................87

## St Stephen's Green

Davy Byrne's ..........................................90

The Duke..................................................94

The Bailey ...............................................98

Kehoe's...................................................102

McDaid's.................................................104

Neary's....................................................108

Shelbourne Hotel....................112

O'Donoghue's .....................................116

Toner's ....................................................120

Doheny and Nesbitt's.......................123

The Bleeding Horse ..........................127

The Portobello ..................................130

## Temple Bar

The Palace ...........................................134

The Oliver St John Gogarty............138

The Auld Dubliner............................141

The Clarence Hotel...........................144

The Norseman ...................................146

## THE NORTHSIDE

The Hole in the Wall......................148

Hanlon's ..............................................152

Gill's ....................................................155

Kavanagh's...........................................157

The Cat and Cage.............................161

The Brian Boru..................................164

Smyth's..................................................168

Clontarf Castle...................................170

Dollymount House...........................174

## THE SOUTHSIDE

The Patriots Inn.................................176

The Penny Black ..............................180

The Morgue........................................182

The Glenside........................................185

## NORTH OF DUBLIN

The Abbey Tavern..............................188

Duffy's ..................................................192

The Lord Mayor's..............................195

The Boot Inn......................................198

The Coachman's Inn .......................202

The Huntsman Inn ..........................205

## SOUTH OF DUBLIN

The Purty Kitchen............................208

The Poitín Stil...................................211

Johnnie Fox's ......................................214

The Roundwood Inn .......................220

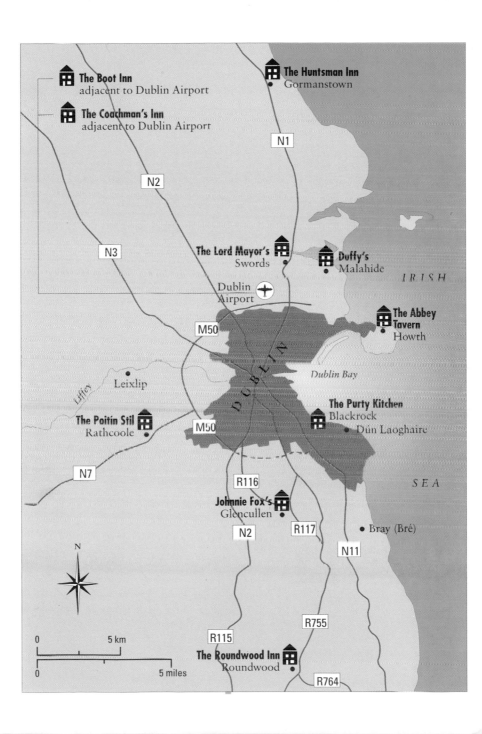

**The Boot Inn**
adjacent to Dublin Airport

**The Coachman's Inn**
adjacent to Dublin Airport

**The Huntsman Inn**
Gormanstown

N1

N2

N3

**The Lord Mayor's**
Swords

**Duffy's**
Malahide

*IRISH*

Dublin
Airport

**The Abbey
Tavern**
Howth

M50

*DUBLIN*

*Dublin Bay*

*Liffey*

Leixlip

**The Purty Kitchen**
Blackrock

Dún Laoghaire

**The Poitín Stil**
Rathcoole

M50

N7

*SEA*

R116

**Johnnie Fox's**
Glencullen

R117

N2

Bray (Bré)

N11

N

R755

0        5 km

R115

0                5 miles

**The Roundwood Inn**
Roundwood

R764

1   THE LORD EDWARD
2   THE CASTLE INN
3   MOTHER RED CAPS
4   THE BRAZEN HEAD
5   THE LONG HALL
6   THE STAG'S HEAD

7   THE OLD STAND
8   GROGAN'S
9   THE INTERNATIONAL
10  O'NEILL'S
11  BOWE'S
12  THE LONG STONE

13  MULLIGAN'S
14  THE OVAL
15  THE FLOWING TIDE
16  THE PARNELL MOONEY
17  PATRICK CONWAY'S
18  NANCY HAND'S

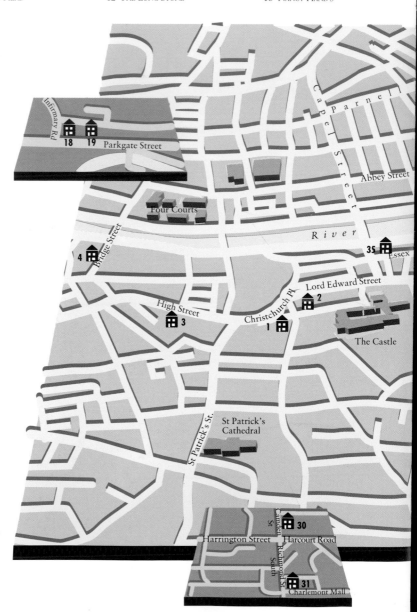

19 RYAN'S OF PARKGATE
20 DAVY BYRNE'S
21 THE DUKE
22 THE BAILEY
23 KEHOE'S
24 McDAID'S

25 NEARY'S
26 SHELBOURNE HOTEL
27 O'DONOGHUE'S
28 TONER'S
29 DOHENY AND NESBITT'S
30 THE BLEEDING HORSE

31 THE PORTOBELLO
32 THE PALACE
33 THE OLIVER ST JOHN GOGARTY
34 THE AULD DUBLINER
35 THE CLARENCE HOTEL
36 THE NORSEMAN

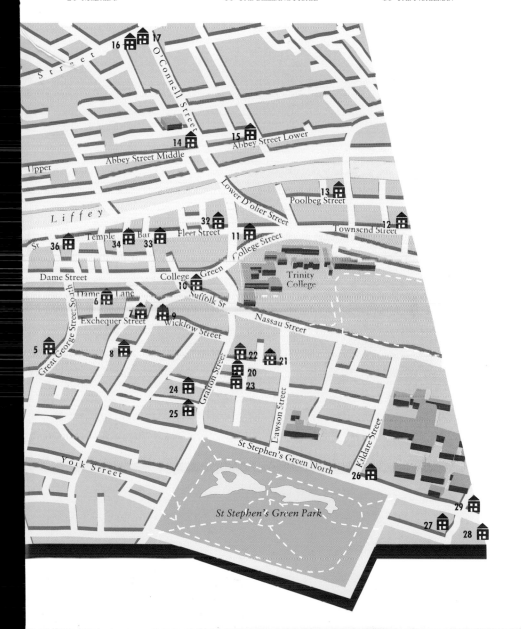

# INTRODUCTION

*Good puzzle would be cross Dublin without passing a pub*

James Joyce, *Ulysses*

*In Dublin you're never more than twenty paces from a pint*

JP Donleavy

The pub in Ireland is as rooted in the national character as the church and, despite their obvious antagonism as rival centres of the community, they have common roots. The tradition of ale brewing in Ireland goes back more than 800 years to the monks of St Francis Abbey in Kilkenny who discovered the best way to combine barley and yeast into a fine brew. (The ruins of their abbey still stand in the grounds of the Smithwick's brewery.) Monks are also credited with pioneering the art of distilling in Ireland as early as the 6th century, having learned such skills from their missionary odysseys around Europe. Whiskey was produced both for recreational purposes and as a medicinal compound; they called it *uisce beatha*, Gaelic for "water of life".

In the Middle Ages most brewing and distilling was done by women in the home; sweet, unhopped ale being the staple table beverage of the time. Those who were best at it went on to transform their homes into inns. On travelling to Dublin in 1610, British pamphleteer Barnaby Rich observed that profit-making in the city revolved almost entirely around alehouses and the selling of ale. At this time Irish brewing and distilling were small scale and still done on the premises where the drinks were sold. A century later, one Sir William Petty estimated that a third of the houses in the city were alehouses. By the late 18th century, Dublin had a population of some 25,000 people, there were some 2000 alehouses, 300 taverns and 1200 brandy shops. The causes of such unnerving statistics were manifold, and included poverty, low excise duty and government aid for the distilling industry.

Distilling and brewing really came into their own

as a commercial concern during the late 18th century. Though there were a host of distillers, whiskey production became heavily dominated by the two big Dublin distillers: Jameson's, established in 1780 and Power's, established in 1791. By the middle of the 19th century whiskey was a vast industry and the staple dinner drink of the majority of the population. The two big brewers by this time were Beamish & Crawford founded in Cork in 1792 and, most famously, Arthur Guinness who started brewing in 1756 and set up at the St James' Gate site in Dublin three years later, taking out a 9000-year lease on the entire property at an annual rent of £45.

Initially Irish brewers produced only ale, but in 1787 Arthur Guinness began to brew porter, a dark beer made with roasted barley. It was first drunk, and given its name, by London's street market porters. It was a cheap and relatively nutritious drink, a perfect quencher for the labouring classes who were the mainstay of Dublin

**Above** Arthur Guinness, founder of the famous Dublin brewing dynasty

# If he can say as you can
# Guinness is good for you
# How grand to be a Toucan
# Just think what Toucan do

**Above** There must be a Guinness toucan somewhere on show in almost every pub in Ireland

pub life. A distinctive Irish style porter soon developed called "stouter porter" (and soon just stout) that used larger quantities of roasted barley to give it the distinctive dark and bitter quality we know today. Since then the drink has gone on to become a national icon as potent as the shamrock and celebrated by everyone from poets to politicians.

Guinness's huge profile is in part due to it being one of the most advertised products in the world. Its famous posters and signs, particularly the many mid-20th-century examples drawn by John Gilroy, have become part of the livery of Irish pubs old and new from Dublin to Frankfurt. Similarly the 19th and early 20th-century signage of Ireland's many distillers – etched mirrors, tin signs and stained glass – is an integral part of the ambience of the traditional Irish pub.

Originally beer and whiskey would have been delivered from the breweries (St James' Gate for Guinness) and distilleries (Power's original premises in John's Lane and Jameson's old Bow Street

**Above** Old Irish ephemera in the window of the Portobello Hotel

distillery) by horse-drawn drays. Both whiskey and beer were delivered in large wooden casks. Beer was served on draught drawn from the casks and also bottled, corked and labelled (with the pub's own name as well as that of the brewer) on the premises for off-licence sales. Whiskey too needed serious attention with publicans bonding it themselves and sometimes blending, colouring and sweetening it too. Some publicans made a name for themselves by their skills with whiskey and drinkers would go out of their way for a particular dram.

**Above** The Power's brand etched in glass at McDaid's

14

The origin of the pub as literally "a public house" is still evident in the ambience and layout of the Irish pub perhaps more than anywhere else in the British Isles. Irish pubs were privately owned. They weren't bound by the kind of brewer-tenant contracts that applied in England. They were bought and sold at public auctions, which copper-fastened their personal aspect. Unlike the English pub, the owner was always the most important element. His was more often than not the name above the door and he set the tone and standards of the establishment. The furnishing was usually domestic and there was little differentiation between the private and public areas of the house. Publicans had strong almost paternal relationships with their regulars, often allowing them to run up an account on a slate if funds were low.

Irish pubs were at the very hub of the community and many had wider roles beyond serving liquid refreshment, being also grocers, general stores, wine and tea merchants and off-licences, with only thin partitions dividing the sale of spices and foodstuffs from that of drink. Some pubs even doubled as local morgues.

**Above** Personal services – Irish pubs commonly take their name from the proprietor

15

Others were coaching inns or taverns that needed to provide food and lodgings for the traveller and stables for their horses. By the Victorian era there were also more cosmopolitan establishments: great palaces rich in architectural splendour both inside and out, with elaborately carved wood, marble, mirror and glasswork all designed to charm the customer and part him from his hard-earned cash.

Opening times varied, although there was a universal "Holy Hour" between 2.30 and 3.30 in the afternoon to give the barmen a break and allow them to clean the premises before the next deluge of drinkers. Some pubs were given special dispensation to open very early in the morning, either to cater for agricultural traders arriving early for markets or, if situated near ports, for dockers on shift-work loading and unloading the ships. So-called "bona fide" taverns were those on the outskirts of the city which had licences to serve beer into the small hours to facilitate thirsty travellers in mid-journey. Ireland being

**Above** Toner's displays its heritage as both a spirit merchants and a literary haunt

Ireland, of course, such privileges were abused by those who weren't on any kind of journey at all except to the pub itself. The rule was that they should have spent the night before three miles away from the pub in question, but of course many people desperate for a drink were willing to travel that three miles with the express purpose of slaking their thirst.

Traditional pubs were primarily patronised by the working classes and many were almost solely a male preserve. In addition to providing a place to drink, they were very much at the social hub of their communities and represented for many a home from home: a place where a man could, for better or worse, forget his domestic responsibilities and his woes at work and, for the price of a drink, put the world to rights in conversation with his neighbour. Then, as now, drink was the great leveller and pubs became poor men's clubs, neutral venues where social standing wasn't so much of an issue as it was in the world outside its doors. Today, in an age when churches and other hallowed meeting places don't attract the numbers they used to, pubs often continue to perform the function of communal sanctuaries. Perhaps with this in mind, Flann O'Brien defined them as "licensed tabernacles". This is the true heart of the Irish pub: something less tangible than carved wood and etched glass. It is a benign mood: sometimes one of quiet reverence and contemplation, sometimes one of lively conversation and greater exuberance (not forgetting that the pub has always been the prime haven for Irish folk music). Whether communicating in words or music, it is what is universally referred to as the *craic*.

Taverns from the 18th century onward were also used as meeting-places for lawyers, politicians and other societies. Under British rule, they were places where local issues were discussed and discontentments aired, and ultimately where grassroot plots against

British imperialism were hatched. Many of the pubs in this book have strong connections with the likes of Wolfe Tone, Charles Stewart Parnell and Michael Collins. Famously, the Dublin pub has provided a home for literary folk. Journalists, poets and writers have used them as informal clubs: places to discuss the matters of the day, places to write in and write about. Pubs are the very stage on which the drama of many an Irish play or novel unfolds: from Joyce and Synge to Flann O'Brien and JP Donleavy.

This book contains a cross-section of pubs which have shaped and been shaped by the cultural, literary, political and historical elements of Ireland's bittersweet past. Most are authentically laid out and preserve their original features, but some of them have compromised their integrity to some extent, either by tarting themselves up to suit elements of the young generation that has more disposable income than sentiment, or by shipping in artefacts by the truckload, providing in quantity what they perhaps lack in quality. Truly historic pubs may be at a premium — in the past decade 20 of the 22 bars in Temple Bar have changed their interiors, which is an ominous statistic. But thankfully the phenomenon of the superpub has so far not become ubiquitous. The number of preservation orders on old pubs is heartening, but many other establishments have already been transformed beyond recognition by unscrupulous developers anxious to seek out the visitor's shilling.

With Ireland's economy booming, there has been a large injection of capital to the licensed trade (not dissimilar to the aforementioned late-Victorian pub boom). Some of this has resulted in changes for the better and some hasn't, but Irish pubs have a reputation for garrulous frivolity and no speculators can take that away. So lift up your glass and raise a toast to those houses of dreams where social divisiveness is blacked out, even if only for the duration of a session.

**Left** The Palace Bar was Flann O'Brien's "licensed tabernacle" of choice

## THE CITY CENTRE

# THE LORD EDWARD

23 CHRISTCHURCH PLACE

These distinguished three-storey late-Victorian premises overlooking Christchurch Cathedral positively reek of history. The pub is built on the historic Wood Quay site that dates back to the Middle Ages. Just up the road, where the charmless modern bunkers of Dublin Corporation's Civic Offices now stand, the remains of a Viking Hiberno-Norman town, dating back to the 10th century, was discovered in the 1970s. There were huge protests against the developers when the proposal of building over this precious site was first mooted, but these protests eventually gave way to the bulldozers. Some of the archaeological discoveries, which included items such as swords, coins and pottery, are now on view in Christchurch and the National Museum.

The pub is named after Lord Edward Fitzgerald, one of the leaders of the republican Irish rebellion of 1798. Fitzgerald is buried in the vault of nearby St Werbergh's Church – on the street of the same name – said to be the oldest church in Dublin, dating back to 1759.

Whatever revamping has been done to the Lord Edward has preserved the essence of the building, outside and in: the floor and wall tiles go back to 1901 and there are stained-glass windows everywhere, as well as lots of panelled snugs, two of which have been fashioned from old entrances to the pub. (There used to be four entrances in all, which is astounding considering the relatively small size

**Right** The Lord Edward – named after the 18th-century rebel leader Edward Fitzgerald

of the place.) In the tiny snug in the corner, privacy is ensured with curtains across trellised windows, and a pulley controls a stained-glass window above – a very old and attractive method of ventilation. Behind the heavy marble counter the shelving suggests that groceries were once sold here as well.

As you ascend the stairs to the upstairs lounge, you have the feeling of being in somebody's house rather than in a public place. The same sense is evident in the lounge itself, with its restrained decor, an open hearth and an attractive white arch decorated with crossed swords. The copper-topped counter has a stained-glass depiction of "The Meeting of the Waters", the confluence of Wicklow's Avonmore and Avonbeg rivers, immortalised in Thomas Moore's poem of the same name. The 1798 theme is reprised here, with sketches of Fitzgerald's arrest and also that of his fellow insurrectionists.

Visitors keen to learn of the local history are advised to ask for regular patron Tom Smith, who, according to popular wisdom, knows more about the area than any guide-book can tell you. There's a picture of his father beside the counter, standing outside what must be the narrowest shop in Ireland. (It measures a mere 7ft in width, Smith's father managing to touch both ends by stretching out his hands.)

Hungry patrons make their way further up to the seafood restaurant, which is very popular with Dublin folk. But if you want to eat on the move, you could sample something from the world-renowned Burdocks fish and chip shop next door.

**Above** Much of the Lord Edward's simple Victorian elegance remains today.

# THE CASTLE INN

5 LORD EDWARD STREET

With its stone walls, open hearth and assorted weaponry studded round the walls, this really does carry the aura of a castle about it. It also has something of a church-like atmosphere, thanks in particular to the presence of an old pulpit across from the counter, though in latter times this has been more often used for DJs to spin records at weekends.

The residence of the Usher family in the 17th century, it afterwards became a coffee house and dram shop. A plaque outside records that the poet James Clarence Mangan — author of powerful ballads and songs like "Dark Rosaleen" — was born here in 1803 . At this time it was a grocery and spirit store run by his father, a cruel man who eventually went bankrupt. Mangan, an occasional librarian at Trinity College, would also die in penury at the age of 46, after a life riddled with depression, alcoholism and opium addiction. His ghost is said to haunt the pub.

The street was once called Fishamble Street, but was renamed at the end of the 19th century after Lord Edward Fitzgerald, the nationalist leader who died after the failure of the Irish rebellion of 1798. Ironically enough, he was betrayed to the British by a man who used to work as a pot-boy here. In the early 1900s Michael Collins, the then treasurer of the Irish Republican Brotherhood, was a regular, an extraordinary venue for him to choose, considering the British stronghold of Dublin Castle was just round the corner. But then the Big Fella always liked to live dangerously.

It's a large pub, but so copiously furnished you're not too aware of this. Apart from the spears and other weaponry, the walls carry provincial shields and a pair of handcuffs, the latter sufficient to remind us that a pillory once stood outside the door.

Though it is well worth a visit, both for its decor and historical connections, the place is partial to loud music at night and has found it necessary to employ bouncers at the door; not because it attracts a rough element, but for insurance purposes.

After you've drunk your fill, you may wish to tour around the area. Not far away is St Patrick's Cathedral, the national cathedral of the Church of Ireland. It was founded in 1190 by John Comyn, the first Englishman to become Archbishop of Dublin, but a church has been on the site since AD450, which makes it the oldest Christian site in Dublin. It was near ruination in 1860 when the Guinness family gave a donation towards its restoration.

Jonathan Swift was Dean of the cathedral from 1713 until his death 32 years later. He campaigned tirelessly – and fiercely – against poverty but also suffered immense agonies within himself; the savage satire of humanity in *Gulliver's Travels* points to his final mental collapse. (It's now thought he may have suffered from Ménière's disease.) Swift is buried in the cathedral beside Esther Johnson, the beloved Stella of his poems. His epitaph reads: "He lies where furious indignation can no longer rend his heart." In his will he left money for the building of a psychiatric institution. This became known as Swift's Hospital but is now called St Patrick's. The sardonic Dean quipped that had he been rich enough, he would have left enough funds for the asylum to cover the whole of Ireland.

**Above** The Castle Inn where Michael Collins was a regular in the 1900s

# MOTHER RED CAPS

CHRISTCHURCH BACK LANE

Many people find it difficult to believe that a shoe factory for the Winstanley chain was once based here, or, more controversially, a brothel. This outsized bar, first established in 1760, reopened in its present form in 1988 and four years later won an award from *The Good Pub Guide*, and it's not hard to see why.

It's a straightforward pub in concept: large but not rambling. You can see it all at a glance – the long counter, a raised area, the open hearth, the snug-like effects. It looks more like a barn than a bar, with its light pine timber procured from an old flour mill – even the light shades have been fashioned from old mill shoots used to drive the grain. Apart from decorative knick-knacks on the shelves (old earthenware pots, decanters, bottles, ceramic statues, china plates and whatnot), everything is wooden: the floors, the ceiling, the furniture. The bench-like tables are scratched and natural, with no attempt at being twee or genteel.

There are so many paintings on display you might feel as if you're in a gallery, and there's a strong republican flavour, with portraits of politicians Charles Stewart Parnell and Michael Davitt. One sketch, carrying the message "The Real Irish Spirit", shows a soldier going off to fight in World War I and a gentleman behind him in civvies saying "I'll go with you", but the bar is much more Easter Rising of 1916 than 1914-18 in tone.

Other displays highlight important dates and events in Ireland's history: a page from the *Cork Free Press* of 1916, another one from the *Limerick Chronicle* of 1922. A passenger sailing timetable of 1900 from

**Left** Mother Red Caps – the premises were once home to a brothel

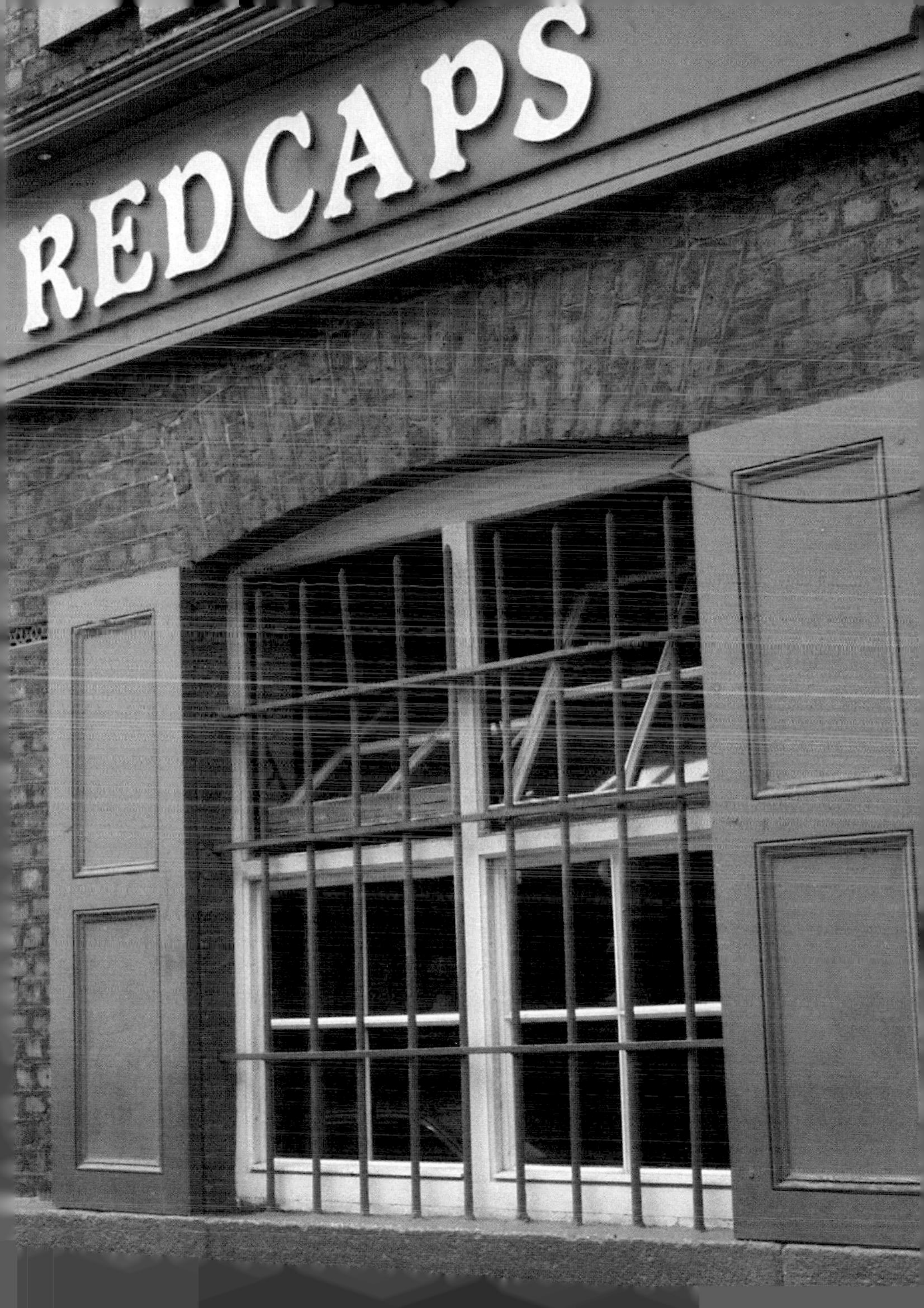
REDCAPS

the Dominion Line Royal and United States Steamers, advertises the route from Queenstown to Boston via the Great Southern and Western Railway. There's also a sketch of Old Mother Red Cap herself, madam of the brothel housed here in the 18th century.

At the other end of the pub we come up to date, with photographs of the likes of Bertie Ahern, the English footballer Jack Charlton (who won the country's heart as Republic of Ireland manager between 1986 and 1996) and musicians Christy Moore and Ronnie Drew. The latter pair may spring to mind if you're here at night, when the place erupts with blues and jazz music.

**Above** The Brazen Head – Dublin's oldest pub

# THE BRAZEN HEAD

20 LOWER BRIDGE STREET

The Brazen Head is Dublin's oldest pub, though it's a matter of some conjecture how much it pre-dates its competitors. A sign outside the door states that it was founded in 1198, but this refers to an earlier tavern built on the same site. Such a detail didn't deter regulars from rowdily celebrating its 800th birthday in 1998. Some people insist there was an inn on the site even before the Norman invasion of 1172. Licensing laws came to Ireland in 1635, and the pub's franchise originally dates from 1666 when Charles II granted the licence. The present building dates from the 1750s.

If you are to visit only one pub in Dublin, make it this one. It was miraculously saved by a preservation order, unlike so many taverns of its vintage that were levelled by bulldozers, and is the only surviving remnant of pre-Augustan Dublin.

The pub is situated on the Quays just across from the Four Courts on the edge of the Liffey's oldest bridge — Father Matthew Bridge. Or, coming from another angle, down the hill from Christchurch. You reach its entrance by walking down an arched alleyway and through a stone-paved courtyard.

It's a dark bar with low ceilings, and you can almost sniff the sense of history upon entry. "Mind your auld head", reads a sign above the door, which looks as if it goes all the way back to 1198.

The antiquarian memorabilia that adorns the place includes old bar price lists on the walls, a housemaid's bell outside the main bar, and engravings on the stair windows. Inside there is currency from all around the world pasted onto the ceiling and also, curiously, an array of American policemen's badges which have been donated by visiting

Yanks over the years.

Its nooks and crannies are beguilingly quaint, as are the fireplaces, the low beams and the smoky ambience. With its dark corners, creaky stairs and uneven floor (the level of the ground dips in the courtyard – an indication of its antiquity), it's simultaneously a fascinating and eerie place for a drink. It resonates with atmosphere and authenticity, having made few concessions to commercialism in its lengthy tenure on the banks of Anna Livia Plurabelle, as Joyce liked to call the Liffey.

The pub was at its height in the mid-17th century, largely thanks to its privileged location. At the time, the bridge was the main crossing point from north to south Dublin – long before O'Connell Bridge attained that particular status.

The United Irishmen used it as a base for their nationalist plotting against British rule. The group's leaders were arrested here in 1797,

**Above and right** The Brazen Head's present structure dates from the 1750s

not having realised that one of their members, an affluent landowner named Thomas Reynolds, was an informer. Those not in the pub at the time were later apprehended, which meant that the insurrection of 1798 had little support from Dublin. After every subsequent insurrection it was raided almost as a matter of course, in an attempt to "round up the usual suspects".

Robert Emmet, one of the group, kept a room on the premises, strategically placed over a passage by the main door so he could vet possible enemies. He also planned the 1803 Rising from here. He tried to capture Dublin Castle, but it was a lacklustre effort and failed miserably. After he was captured, he was sentenced to hang outside St Catherine's Church in Thomas Street. Before the execution was carried out, he gave his famous "Speech from the Dock" which is presented in full on one of the walls here. The man who hanged him actually used to drink here as well. After he had done his job, some patrons of the Head, with (literal) gallows humour, used to watch him drinking and ask for their drink to be served "from the hangman's glass". Emmet's ghost is said to roam about the place late at night.

Emmet's writing desk was once the pub's proudest exhibit, but it's no longer on the premises. "People come in here and expect to be shown the desk," says the barman, "but business has to compete with history." The compromise is that his seat is viewable, even if the room has been transformed into a (very attractive) restaurant.

Author Eamon Mac Thomáis put it well when he said, "Revolution kept [the pub] in business but also nearly put it out of business". The armed struggle brought it patronage but also resulted in much physical damage to it. It was almost destroyed in the Easter Rising of 1916 and also during the Civil War in 1922, when British artillery shook it to its foundations.

James Joyce mentions the pub grudgingly in *Ulysses* when he has

Corley emote, "You get a decent enough do at the Brazen Head for a bob" (a "do" being a party and a "bob" a shilling). Joyce gets the location wrong, placing it in the nearby Winetavern Street. This was a rare example of memory failing him – it was his boast that if Dublin were ever destroyed by a bomb, it could be rebuilt brick by brick if an architect used *Ulysses* as his template.

Today the pub is frequented by a motley crew of foreign students, dyed-in-the-wool Dubliners, serious Guinness tipplers (they keep a good pint), the old stock and people who have a *grá* – a liking – for traditional music, which is played here frequently.

Lunches are served daily in the carvery bar, which specialises in Irish country recipes.

**Above** The Brazen Head has changed little since the days of the United Irishmen

# THE LONG HALL

51 GREAT GEORGES STREET SOUTH

Not only is the hall lengthy, the pub also has one of the longest counters in Dublin. In times past the main hall itself was the sole preserve of men – women, as elsewhere, took their tipple in the snug – but now the distinctions are thankfully more blurred. The building backs on to Dublin Castle and is claimed to be more than 300 years old, but the present façade suggests it was rebuilt in the mid-19th century. The pub was closed down briefly in 1867 during a witch-hunt for Fenian insurrectionists.

The awnings could do with a bit of freshening up, as could the neighbouring buildings, but once you get inside you forget such minor details. The Long Hall has resolutely refused to re-invent itself for the whims of fashion. It has retained its filigree-edged mirrors, crystal chandeliers and a pendulum clock that's 250 years old. An elaborate wooden arch inlaid with stained glass and a double-faced clock separates the bar from the lounge. Elsewhere lining the walls there are pewter pitchers and brass jugs, portraits of historical figures and paintings of Japanese ladies, some of them in cameo form. Here and there a pair of rifles lie across them, looking very stately indeed in their coat-of-arms fashion.

On the wall a poem by one John Strevell praises the decor, which, he writes, takes us back to a time of "waltzes and wine". The lanterns, the gilded mirrors and the half-panelled walls create an atmospheric effect. It's a dark pub, and some of the paintings on the walls are rather dour, but it also has the air of being a place where one can escape to and commune with the past. The carpet may have seen better days, but even this, and the red velvet chairs, reinforce the same effect.

In the 1920s the Long Hall became an informal meeting place for painters and decorators. The Painter's Union was nearby, but more painters found employment within these walls than anywhere else. Word flew around the pub as to what jobs were coming up, and whoever got the contract would be gratefully replenished with free pints from his mates if they were co-opted as assistants on the job. Those who didn't play the game risked being ignored when the work was handed out.

More contemporary visitors to the pub have included Phil Lynott, who shot one of his videos on the premises, and even a flying visit from Mo Mowlam. Many tourists come here, if only to say they've "done" the Long Hall, but they're easy to tell from the working-class stalwarts who have always proved the mainstay of this most evocative of pubs.

**Above and next page** The Victorian spendour of the Long Hall

# THE STAG'S HEAD

I DAME COURT

For any lover of the Victorian pub in all its opulent excess, the Stag's Head is an essential port of call. It was built in 1770 but re-modelled in 1895 at the height of the Victorian pub building boom, and is a model of its type: bottle-glass windows, wrought-iron chandeliers, carved partitions, plush red-leather seating and bevelled mirrors rising all the way to the ceiling. Glowering down are the eponymous mounted heads, carrying just the right degree of imperiousness. The long mahogany counter, topped with red Connemara marble and sectioned off by glass partitions, was also a popular feature of pubs of this vintage. Rather than the spartan decoration of earlier pubs, the late Victorian pub was aspirational, competing with the grandeur of theatre foyers and the finest gentlemen's clubs in its look; while the partitions offered privacy to middle class customers who would prefer not to be seen in a public house.

James Joyce drank here. It has featured in several films as well. It's also rumoured (or maybe boasted) that American director Quentin Tarantino was refused a drink after hours one night because he tried to pull rank.

**Opposite and above** The Stag's Head is a shrine to Victorian opulence

And you don't pull rank in the Stag's Head because ... well, you just don't. The pub has also been featured on a postage stamp, the ultimate seal of approval by the powers-that-be. Another distinction is that there's a pavement mosaic of it in Dame Street, which is the kind of advertising you just can't pay for these days.

It can get cramped here at times, but this increases the period feel and intimacy. Outside is a shopping arcade generally throbbing with life, and selling everything from sewing needles to anchors, antiques, rare posters and second-hand books. The food is another draw to the pub, in a way that would have been unthinkable in yesteryear, when people came to places like this for one purpose only. Especially popular among regular patrons are the Irish stew and the bacon and cabbage.

**Above** The look aspires to the luxury of a 19th-century gentleman's club

# THE OLD STAND

37 EXCHEQUER STREET

These premises have been licensed since the 16th century, but such a licence hasn't been continuous. The present building, though, is still over 200 years old. Thomas J Ryan, a tea, wine and spirit merchant as well as a grocer, bought it in the early 1900s. It was known as a "safe house" for the likes of Michael Collins and members of the Irish Republican Brotherhood, who often holed up here when they were on the run. (Collins' offices were only a few doors away.)

Now owned by the Dorans, who also run Davy Byrne's, it has an impressive black exterior ringed with gold lettering. Inside there's a horseshoe bar containing a Welsh dresser made of Austrian wood. The back bar is on a raised level behind it. The pub's current name is taken from a portion of a nearby rugby ground that, alas, no longer exists. The bar still has a strong sporting clientele and a fair degree of male bonding – fine if you're part of it, it can be irksome if you aren't. But in general it's a pleasant haven in which to while away the hours.

One of the present bar's most famous regulars in the early 1800s was barrister and wit John Philpott Curran. (He was the father of Sarah Curran, the sweetheart of the famous Irish patriot Robert Emmet.) If that's not good enough for you, London's late Soho reprobate, turf journalist and incorrigible sozzler Jeffrey Bernard once called the Old Stand his favourite bolthole in the British Isles. High praise indeed from somebody who ought to have known about such matters.

Today it's a mecca for the horsey set, the old-school-tie brigade and the ageing jocks who damage their blood pressure discussing scorelines of rugby games most sane people have long since forgotten.

**Next page** The Old Stand – a seasoned sportman's repair

# GROGAN'S

15 WILLIAM STREET SOUTH

*We sat in Grogan's with our faded overcoats finely disarrayed on easy chairs in the mullioned snug. I gave a shilling and two pennies to a civil man who brought us in return two glasses of black porter.*

Flann O'Brien, *At Swim-Two-Birds*

Before the now sadly missed Dublin gent Paddy O'Brien became manager here in the early 1970s, he had worked for 35 years as a barman in McDaid's. O'Brien had always loved the literary ferment created in McDaid's and when it went up for sale in 1972 he put in a bid for it. He didn't think he would have any competition, but at the auction a British lady who owned a number of pubs and wanted to add a literary haunt to her collection, kept matching his price. In the end he had to drop out of the bidding.

O'Brien's friend Tommy Smith had just bought Grogan's pub on the very same day and offered him the job of managing it. O'Brien accepted his offer and brought the literati from McDaid's with him. Brendan Behan, Patrick Kavanagh and Flann O'Brien were all dead by now, but the likes of Ben Kiely, Michael Hartnett, Liam O'Flaherty, Macdara Woods and Tony Cronin all followed O'Brien to Grogan's in what was termed "the flight of the faithful". It could never reprise the magic of McDaid's in the preceding decades, but O'Brien had at least trumped the Auld Enemy. "So she never got her literary pub!" he proclaimed with much satisfaction as he took up his new post here.

Grogan's is also known as the Castle Lounge, after its gable which runs onto Castle Market, where you may well see buskers plying their trade. Further on down is the Georges Street Market, where you can

**Right** Grogan's – perfectly suited to those who favour quiet conversation

Toska

ACTION

Mark Leria

THE
CASTLE
LOUNGE
J. GROGAN

15  J. GROGAN. 15

buy miscellaneous curios. Despite being situated in the heart of a built-up area, the pub exhibits an air of leisurely grandeur. The atmosphere is hushed and refined, and ideally suited to *tête-à-têtes*. Grogan's wears the patina of its years well, and has fought the good fight against neon and plastic, retaining its traditional furniture and fittings. It's the perfect place to retire to with the Sunday supplements for a good read in peace.

The only concession to the present seems to be the modern art exhibits on the walls. These join portraits of notable Irish figures such as the late actor Donal McCann and a stained-glass composition of literary icons at the back of the bar. There is neither television nor jukebox. Tommy Smith, who still owns the pub, describes it as being "like anyone's sitting-room". A member of the Council of Poetry of Ireland, he's always made it his business to try and attract customers who have more to occupy their minds than the next football match. He also rails frequently against the phenomenon of the "superpub" with its eyes squarely fixed on the "main chance".

Grogan's is just a stone's throw away from the fashionable Powerscourt Centre, a collection of cafés, shops, wine bars and restaurants set on three levels in the enclosed, glass-roofed central courtyard of a fine Georgian house. Once the home of the 18th-century Viscount Powerscourt, the house has been carefully preserved, right down (or rather up) to the stucco ceiling. Also nearby is the Dublin Civic Museum, a treasure-trove of memorabilia relating to the city's past. Here, in addition to a collection of Viking artefacts, is the "head" of English naval hero Admiral Nelson, which was severed from his statue in 1966 when the IRA blew up the pillar erected in his memory.

# THE INTERNATIONAL

23 WICKLOW STREET

In 1886 this building was converted from a hostel to a pub and little has changed since then. Okay, so the counter was pulled back a few feet (even now it looks narrow – God only knows what it must have been like a century ago) and the ceiling is coloured nicotine instead of magnolia, but as soon as you walk in the door you feel as if you're taking a trip back in time.

There are a few antiquarian oddments, such as oak casks from which porter was served until the 1940s, and impressive carved figures of river gods, but the place hasn't been prettified, and some may even find it dour. As was the case in many other pubs, women weren't served in

**Above** The International has a reputation for music and comedy

the bar until the early 1970s. The snugs are now gone, sadly, but space would have been something of a problem had they been preserved.

Dotted about are pictures of the pub as it used to look in the 1940s, and an original gold-plated Power's Whiskey mirror reputed to be worth in the region of £7000. Stained glass abounds everywhere, including on the door. There are mirrors and clocks all over the place too, looking equally quaint. The original brass pumps were put back some years ago as well. Old copper pans hang upside down over the counter, and the ceiling is, of all things, papier mâché.

Today the International's main reputation rests on its music and comedy. (In a typical piece of International Bar lunacy, the Comedy Cellar is upstairs, not down.) It's the longest-running comedy venue in Dublin, having started back in the mid-1980s. Indeed, it was here that Ardal O'Hanlon, of television's *Father Ted* fame, cut his stand-up teeth, along with colleagues Kevin Gildea and Dermot Carmody. In February 1988, O'Hanlon faced a live audience for the first time. "I trembled for about 10 minutes. It went well, but I was wetting myself. The audience were very tolerant because they realised it was a first night. Then the following week we went on again. In fact we told the same jokes for five years to the same audience and they still came back for more. They were masochists!" His average weekly wage for such exertions was about £12. Just about enough, as one of his colleagues put it, for "spuds, rice and Bovril".

The affection many feel for the pub is encapsulated by stand-up comic Alex Lyons, who was given a Lifetime Achievement Award by the Cellar: "It's given a platform to so many and it's totally unpretentious. It's never been into money so there's a bit of magic about it, a bit of pedigree. If it was a theatre, it would have produced Liam Neeson and Gabriel Byrne. It's an extraordinary record for a small room above a pub".

**Left** The International was converted from a hostel into a pub in 1886

# O'NEILL'S

2 SUFFOLK STREET

Trinity College, situated opposite O'Neill's on College Green, is the oldest university in Ireland, founded by Elizabeth I in 1592 on the site of a monastery. Her motive, she said, was to create a university that wouldn't be infected by popery. It covers 40 acres and is immensely popular with visitors, who marvel at the cobblestoned Front Square with its large Bell Tower (the Campanile). Former graduates include Oliver Goldsmith, John Millington Synge, Samuel Beckett, Robert Emmet, Wolfe Tone, Oliver St John Gogarty, Bram Stoker, Thomas Moore and Thomas Davis. It featured in the

**Above** The name O'Neill first appeared above the door in 1927

54

film *Educating Rita*, doubling as an English university on that occasion. James Joyce described the place chillingly in *A Portrait of the Artist as a Young Man* as being "set heavily in the city's ignorance like a dull stone set in a cumbrous ring".

Trinity used to be the particular preserve of Protestants; in the 1920s Catholics had to apply for a special dispensation to study there, and free education was offered to Catholics who converted to Protestantism. Such a system prevailed into the modern age, but in 1970 the Catholic church lifted its boycott and no longer was it deemed a mortal sin for Catholics to attend. Today some 70 per cent of students are Catholic.

The main tourist attraction in TCD, to use the building's abbreviation, is the Book of Kells, the beautifully ornate 680-page copy of the gospels written in Latin. This was perhaps the apogee of

Irish art in the aftermath of the Dark Ages when Irish monks proselytised all over Europe. Disputes still rage as to where it was written and designed (it could have been Ireland or Scotland) but it was brought to a monastery in Kells, County Meath, during the Viking raids of the 9th century. It's separated into four vellum volumes but only two are visible at any one time, and only two pages of each. The pages are turned

**Above** The magnificent, ornate wooden backfitting still on show at O'Neill's

periodically, the manuscript itself being preserved in a glass case. It's kept in the Colonnade Gallery on the ground floor of the library. Here you may also see a harp carried into battle by Brian Boru, the Irish chief who ruled over Ireland from 1002 until his death in 1014.

On nearby Grafton Street is a statue of one of Dublin's best-loved ladies, the legendary Molly Malone, "the tart with the cart" from the eponymous folk song. Nobody is quite sure if she sold fish or something more promiscuous but she'll always have a special place in the hearts of Dubliners as she wheels her wheelbarrow "through streets broad and narrow, crying 'cockles and mussels, alive, alive-o'". And this piece of street sculpture – erected in 1988 as part of Dublin's millennial celebrations – is a fitting tribute to her.

Of interest too is the nearby Bank of Ireland on College Green, which was originally the Irish House of Parliament. Built in 1729, it was bought by the bank after the 1800 Act of Union with Britain removed the power of self-government from the Irish.

Going much further back, it was in this area that the Norsemen too held their parliament in the 11th century – or, as they called it, their *thing mote*, from the Norse for assembly place. This was a large mound, some 40ft high and 240ft in circumference, used for public meetings, elections and hangings.

O'Neill's mock-Tudor frontage dates from the late 19th century, but there's been a tavern on this site for over 300 years; the O'Neill name first appeared above the door in 1927. Students and stockbrokers crush together in this throbbing premises, which is really five interconnecting bars for the price of one. You can never be sure if the person sitting next to you will be contemplating their navel or the Dow Jones index. You'll also see a fair share of foreign visitors nipping in for a quick one.

Elegant in style, it has a profusion of wood in its cavernous interior. Every time you turn a corner a new lounge seems to erupt from nowhere, each equally appetising. Then you go upstairs and another one presents itself. There are glass-panelled snugs, stained-glass effects, mirror murals and fireplaces. An air of controlled chaos is in evidence as barmen flit back and forth with trays of food and drink, and customers enter and leave on a kind of revolving-door basis. The conversation is always lively and varied, with maverick and mercurial souls holding forth on the issues of the day. It's not a pretentious place, however, being easy both on the eye and ear.

# BOWE'S

31 FLEET STREET

This elegant establishment is one of the last and certainly best-preserved Victorian pubs in central Dublin. Dating back to an era when manners were more gentle than they are today, it has retained both a genial ethos among its patrons and the essence of its original architecture.

There's a preservation order over the exterior, which features the kind of intricate fresco work all too rare today: a bird-and-grapes motif on green pillars. Also here is the now famous double-sided triangular clock which is still wound manually. According to barman James Murphy, who has been serving pints here for almost two decades now, Bowe's has featured in almost as many books about clocks as about pubs.

Inside, hand-crafted mahogany panels on the walls are covered in ornate mirrors and attractively lit. The counter runs down the right of the bar. Behind it sit two coach lights from old horse-drawn hearses. Many lucrative offers have been put in for these but they aren't budging. Surrounding them is some more intricate fresco work.

The pub opened in 1854, when it was known as Christopher McCabe's, that gentleman being its first landlord. At this time, it was also a lodging-house. The next landlord went one better, turning it into a hotel. In the 1880s it passed into the hands of John O'Connor, and it was under his stewardship that it started to attract customers from the *Irish Times*, which is situated just across the road. Journalists used their offices' rear exit (which was then sandwiched between Jim O'Hara's Billiard Rooms and Amelia Barker's Temperance Hotel) to nip in and wet their lips.

By the 1920s it had earned the reputation of being a "thinking man's pub", a distinction it still enjoys as denizens from "The Old Lady of D'Olier Street" (to use the *Times'* affectionate nickname) continue to visit it for both business and pleasure.

**Above** Bowe's – a fine, well-preserved Victorian establishment

# THE LONG STONE

## 10 TOWNSEND STREET

It was on this precise site that in AD837 the Norsemen landed after blazing a trail across the seas from Scandinavia. They erected a tall stone pillar in the sea, as was the custom, to symbolise their control over a given area. It's from this that the present pub gets its name. The sea is no longer here due to the land reclamation programme of 1663, but the long stone itself, or "steyne" as it was called, stood here until 1794. A modern-day

**Above** The Long Stone was founded in 1754

representation of it is still visible at the front of Pearse Street garda station a few hundred yards away.

The pub was established in 1754 and has passed through many hands since. The Tivnan family took it over in 1994 and refurbished it along ambitious and novel lines. As you walk in the door you're struck by the brownstone walls which have been washed with floating plaster to give a rough-hewn effect, and hieroglyphic-like images bring to mind ancient papyrus texts, or even cave paintings. On the right is a wooden structure that came from a church in England, and at the back bar is the pub's *pièce de résistance*: a massive sculpted head of Bolder, the Viking god of warmth, made from fibreglass but with bricks and mortar on the bottom half, which has been cast in clay. Inside Bolder's wide-open mouth is the pub's hearth, making it look as if he's breathing fire.

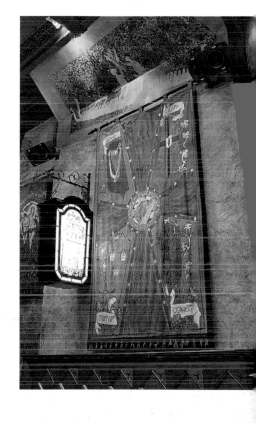

The *Irish Press* offices used to be nearby, so there are old newspapers in the downstairs snug to nudge some nostalgia, and elsewhere are old tins of Gold Flake and Sweet Afton tobacco, numerous bottles of Guinness and rare old books open at selected pages. Beside a very impressive wood structure, which was carved with chainsaws from a dead tree, is a wooden arch which leads you to the upstairs bar.

**Above** The interior decor plays up the pub's ancient affiliations.

The ceiling seems very far away, lit from skylights.

Upstairs are more curiosities: an old Royal typewriter on a table, a frieze on the wall featuring a couple wearing not much more than fig leaves and carrying the ironic title "Amalgamated Society of Tailors". Other friezes scattered throughout carry mercurial messages. "Down with Unionist strength!" says one; another quotes from Sean O'Casey's play *The Plough and the Stars*: "The great are not great. The great only appear great because we are on our knees."

The clientele comprises the business community who come to sample the appetising carvery lunches, but the Long Stone's proximity to Trinity College makes it popular with the younger set as well. At night it throbs with energy (there's frequent live music) and, as you stride across the stained-wood floor and explore its many nooks, you can imagine how the Vikings must have felt as they took root here, making decisions on their *thing mote* – another term for the mound of earth round the steyne which was a kind of Viking parliament – that would affect generations to come.

All in all, it's a totally pleasurable experience to sit here and browse or daydream. The staff are extremely friendly and the menu on offer – at very keen prices – would whet anybody's palate. Make it a must.

**Above** A Viking god fireplace helps keep Long Stone customers warm in winter

# MULLIGAN'S

8 POOLBEG STREET

A classic Dublinesque pub and a Dublin institution. Mulligan's was established in 1782 and since then has stoutly — forgive the pun — resisted selling out to the speculator's shilling, making few concessions to modernity in its lengthy tenure in the heart of the city.

The Liffey literally ran outside its doors before Dublin was walled in, a fact attested to by the name of the street in which it's situated: *poolbeg* translated from the Gaelic means "little pool". The present building dates from the 1850s, and has seen a motley crew of patrons come and go in its time.

For a while it used to be the haunt of thirsty thespians from the Old Theatre Royal, where figures such as Bing Crosby and Gracie Fields once appeared. That building was knocked down in 1962, however, and replaced with the soulless monstrosity that is Hawkins House office block, one of the ugliest buildings in the city.

The late barman Paddy Flynn, who served his first pint here in 1925, said the pulling down of that theatre caused him much chagrin. When it was there, he could hear the hammering in of the stage sets. Many British stars frequented the pub when they were appearing in the Royal in revues, and Paddy was amused by their cockney accents.

Paddy remembered a time when keeping bar in Dublin was a much more demanding trade. As well as serving the punters, a barman had to rack and bond the whiskey: colouring and sweetening it in the barrel with burnt sugar (whiskey often arrived from the distillery as a clear spirit) and then bottling it with their own labels. "These days," on the contrary, "everything is just dumped on the counter," making life a whole lot easier.

At first Paddy lived on the premises but eventually he bought himself a house in Mountjoy Square for £198. In the early years, he worked 12 hours a day for six days a week, pocketing a weekly salary of just £1. You couldn't get up to much mischief on £1, even in those days. The political climate was another disincentive to going out. There were frequently 9pm curfews at times of trouble. Before Paddy's time, the pub had also seen raids by the brutal Black and Tan auxiliary police force; these former servicemen were sent from Britain to assist the Royal Irish Constabulary, who were under attack from the Irish Republican Army.

Paddy once had a patron he never forgot: a young man who rambled in one day with a couple of other fellows and ordered a bottle of beer. He was a newspaper man just out of the army, and he went by the name of John Fitzgerald Kennedy. "I had no idea," Paddy said later, "that I was looking at the future president of the United States." When Kennedy returned to Ireland in 1962 on an official visit, Paddy enquired through official channels if there was a possibility he might return to the pub. Time constraints made that impossible, but Paddy got a lovely reply saying JFK hoped to make it back some time in the future. But of course that would never happen: in November 1963, he was assassinated.

Mulligan's is a noisy pub, positively churning with energy when it's packed. In the old days a group calling itself (ahem) "The Society for the Preservation of the Dublin Accent" used to meet here. Their work wasn't in vain, if the guttural sounds of hardened drinkers calling for another pint of Guinness are anything to go by. Many people say the pub serves the best pint of Guinness in the country; it has many competitors in this department, some of which are located within spitting distance of the brewery itself, but you may well get a funny look from the barman if you don't order this brew.

**Above** Mulligan's immaculately preserved exterior

Originally, the proprietors used to bottle their own beer in the basement. It was also a so-called "market house", which meant it was allowed open earlier than the other pubs in the area to cater for the early-rising market traders without infringing the licensing laws.

When James Mulligan took over he banned stools and chairs from the pub, being of the opinion that real men should stand up as they drank. The last of the Mulligan clan to have a hand in the pub, James Mulligan, died in 1932. The pub was then taken over by Mick Smith who died in 1962, leaving it to his nephews who still run it. There's no food on offer, making it clear that it's a place for the seriously committed drinker. The little back room, with its large central table,

**Above** The stark elegance of Mulligan's back room

looks more suited to company AGMs than boozing sessions. The pub featured in James Joyce's *Dubliners* story "Counterparts", a sad tale in which Farrington, a disgruntled clerk, holes up in the back parlour of the pub, frittering away the money he's received from pawning his watch on drink and fair-weather friends. More recently the bar was used as a location for the filming of Christy Brown's autobiography *My Left Foot*.

The pub's best-loved client is undoubtedly sportswriter Con Houlihan, who spent years here dropping pearls of wisdom about life, literature and football. He worked for most of his life in the offices of the *Evening Press* round the corner, until it shut down in the early 1990s. He had looked on the newspaper as a home from home, and Mulligan's as a second one.

There's a plaque to him on the wall, with tributes from playwright John B Keane and poet and fellow-countyman Brendan Kennelly. "I played rugby *against* him and drank porter *with* him," Keane writes. "We were useful enough players, but we excelled at the other." Of Con's writing, Keane says: "When he entered the sporting scene the cobwebs of bias and bigotry were blown away by the pure breath of his vision and honesty." Kennelly adds that he's "a big man with a sharp eye who sees into the hearts of men." He also has some unique drinking habits, one of which is to put milk in his brandy.

Con can't get here as much as he would like these days, and his absence may be symbolic of a seismic shift in the clientele in general. Its patrons today comprise the staff of the aforementioned Hawkins House and the Central Bank, also nearby. Such patrons are a far cry from the primarily working-class customers it once attracted.

Some cynics have accused Mulligan's of having an air of *negligentia diligens*, of studied disorder, but this isn't so. It has always been itself, for good or ill.

# THE OVAL

78 MIDDLE ABBEY STREET

Before entering the pub, have a look around the corner at Dublin's General Post Office, or the GPO as it's more often called, a fine granite building (built c.1815) with an Ionic portico and six fluted columns outside. The nationalist heroes of the Easter Rising of 1916 used it as their headquarters when they launched their insurrection.

Easter Monday was chosen as the day for the rising because all the military would be at the races. Union leader James Connolly led the Irish Citizen Army and Patrick Pearse the Irish Republican Brotherhood. Together they took possession of a number of key buildings. They barricaded themselves into the GPO and it was almost destroyed in the subsequent fighting. Only the façade remained after it was shelled by an English gunboat from the Liffey. It was also badly shelled during the civil war of 1922. It was subsequently restored and re-opened in 1929; yet it still bears the marks of bullets on its walls.

Pearse read out a Declaration of Independence which he hoisted upon the tricolour in his proudest moment. Within a week, however, British troops captured all the rebels. Their execution galvanised public sympathy for their cause much more than the rising itself could ever have hoped to do, and made martyrs of them. Public outrage was particularly strong over the shooting of James Connolly, who had been badly injured during the fighting and had to be tied to a chair as he was executed.

Just inside the GPO is a beautiful marble statue of the mythological Irish martyr Cuchulainn. He's reputed to have tied himself to a pillar after he was wounded so he could face his enemies even in death. Only when a raven – the harbinger of death – settled on his shoulder did they dare approach. On the plinth is the Declaration of Independence with its seven signatories.

Also in O'Connell Street is the much-hyped "floozie in the jacuzzi", a bronze statue of James Joyce's personification of the Liffey, Anna Livia. It's also irreverently known as "the whore in the sewer" (this one only works with a good Dub accent). It was built in 1988 to commemorate Dublin's millennium. The site chosen was the place previously occupied by Nelson's Pillar, a statue erected to Admiral Nelson in 1815 to commemorate the British hero's victory over the French at Trafalgar.

The column was damaged irreparably by an IRA bomb in 1966, the 50th anniversary of the 1916 Rising, and had to be destroyed. (A subsequent riddle went: "What's the difference between Napoleon and Nelson?

Napoleon was Bonaparte and Nelson was blown apart".) Afterwards, a certain degree of sadness was felt by those who used the spot as a meeting-place. "See you at the Pillar!" was the cry of a whole generation who had scant regard for Nelson's politics, or indeed his

**Above** The rebuilt Oval – the original premises were destroyed in the Easter Rising

nationality. Ironically, the more "patriotic" fountain seems to have garnered little or no respect, and is more frequently used as a rubbish bin than a place of reverence.

O'Connell Street also has a statue of James Larkin (1876–1947), the man who spearheaded the trade union movement in Ireland. The most impressive statue of all, however, is that of Catholic politician Daniel O'Connell (1775–1847), which features him towering above various figures of Irish society. Underneath these are four winged creatures representing Fidelity, Courage, Eloquence and Patriotism: qualities all embodied by O'Connell. The statue took nearly 20 years to build, being finally unveiled in 1882.

Further on up O'Connell Street is the Gresham Hotel, which dates from 1817. The original building was destroyed in the Civil War in 1922 but it has been rebuilt and extensively renovated many times since then. At the top of the street is the Ambassador Cinema, which was once part of the Rotunda Hospital complex.

Also nearby is Dublin's main Catholic church, the Pro-Cathedral, built between 1816 and 1825. It was originally intended for O'Connell Street, but members of the Protestant ascendancy objected to it holding such a high-profile location, so it was built on what is now called Cathedral Street instead. It has a Doric exterior (the six columns are modelled on the Temple of Theseus in Athens) and a domed Renaissance interior.

Located behind the church at the turn of the 19th century, with typical Irish incongruity, was Dublin's red-light district. The area was known as "Monto" or, as James Joyce called it in *Ulysses*, "Nighttown". In the early 1920s more than 1500 prostitutes plied their trade here, but pressure from the church in 1925 caused them all to be finally driven off the streets. Former brothels were subsequently "blessed" with holy pictures in makeshift rituals of would-be exorcism.

There's been a pub here since 1820. Fifty years later, it was selling groceries and tobacco as well. It acquired its present name in 1904, was destroyed during the Easter Rising of 1916 and rebuilt in the 1920s. Its most eccentric proprietor of that time, James Browne, insisted on wearing a bowler hat behind the counter at all times.

It's now frequented by a diverse set of customers ranging widely across the socio-political divide. Journalists, civil servants, legal eagles, those from the film world, they've all stopped here to do business, parley or relax. The pub was even more of a hubbub when O'Connell Street – one of the widest streets in Europe – was the centre of the city's activity. It has fallen from grace somewhat in the past few decades and has let itself go to an extent, parts of it having become rather tacky. (It is also something of a no-go area late at night from a crime standpoint).

The *Independent* newspaper offices are a few doors down, so its journalists tend to drop in between shifts to slake their thirst – and perhaps survey the many sketches of past employees of their newspaper that grace the walls. There are also framed editions of old "Indo" papers, including the one commemorating its 30th anniversary in 1935. (The theme continues in the upstairs restaurant, neatly arranged with circular tables and again awash with sketches of journalistic personages on the walls.)

Decoratively, its other appurtenances are perhaps of the type that is *de rigueur* in "quaintified" pubs these days: large brass pitchers, clocks, a sewing machine and typewriter. More impressive is the large harp that sits in the window. There's also a tiny snug where you'll see a chart of the itinerary taken by Leopold Bloom in *Ulysses*: Joyce mentions the bar in the Wandering Rocks episode, where Mr Daedalus drinks with Ned Lambert. (Samuel Beckett, who was once secretary to Joyce, features it in his early collection of stories, *More Pricks than Kicks*.)

# THE FLOWING TIDE

9 ABBEY STREET LOWER

Dating back to 1824 but having gone through many refurbishments since then, the Flowing Tide is not what you'd call a "happening" pub. It's decidedly untouristy, and bereft of the kind of flashy gimmicks more trendy establishments employ to attract the the floating drinker. Having said that, it's far from a spit-and-sawdust pub. With a central bar and neatly wooded-off partitions, it's amiably leisurely — and refreshingly unself-conscious.

The fact that it's situated across the road from the Abbey Theatre

**Above** Across from the Abbey Theatre, the Flowing Tide has seen its share of thespians

means it has played host to more than a few thespians. The late lamented Donal McCann drank here, as did a slew of his colleagues and co-stars, many of whom are featured in wall sketches. Playwright Tom Murphy is also an aficionado. Indeed there's a portrait of him on the wall, quoting him saying that Ireland was "a pain in the arse" to him when he was growing up in the 1950s, and also, more significantly, "I cannot separate my life from my association with the Abbey." Elsewhere are stained-glass panels with a literary/stage theme, and a large portrait of Samuel Beckett. The pub also has a large sporting following, and sportswriter Con Houlihan (*see* Mulligan's) often drank here when he was working with the Press Group. Politics is another topic much discussed among the imbibers. (Another wall carries a touching picture of US president John F Kennedy's 1962 visit to Ireland.)

The Abbey Theatre itself was co-founded in 1904 by WB Yeats (who contributed his own plays for performance), Lady Augusta Gregory and Edward Martyn, and spearheaded the Irish Literary Renaissance. Since then it has staged many plays by seminal theatrical figures such as George Moore, Brian Friel, John B Keane, Hugh Leonard and Frank McGuinness. The theatre was destroyed by fire in 1951 but was rebuilt in the 1960s. It now houses a second auditorium, which stages productions of lesser known dramatists.

The Abbey predated the 1916 uprising by only a little more than a decade. Clearly, it paved the way for a shifting in the political goalposts in giving the Irish a sense of cultural pride. The establishment of the political party *Sinn Féin* (Gaelic for "we ourselves" or "we alone") followed soon afterwards, advocating economic and cultural self-sufficiency for Ireland and a boycott of the British Parliament. Yeats didn't ally himself to this, having mixed feelings about the "terrible beauty" of republicanism.

One of the busiest nights in the pub's (and the Abbey's) history took place in 1907 when riots broke out after the theatre staged JM Synge's *The Playboy of the Western World*, which contained some profanities Irish audiences weren't willing to take on board. Nine years later it was again rocked, this time more literally, when a British battleship, the *HMS Helga*, started shelling the nationalist rebels stationed in the General Post Office. Some of the shells fell short and one of them landed here, almost destroying the building.

Another eventful night in the Flowing Tide's colourful history took place in 1926 when riots again broke out in the Abbey after the staging of Sean O'Casey's *The Plough and the Stars*, a play which revised the notion of Irish womanhood, as well as casting a dim light over certain aspects of republicanism. Outraged audiences bayed for O'Casey's blood and Yeats tried vainly to placate them with words. "You have disgraced yourselves again. Is this going to be a recurring celebration of Irish genius? First Synge, then O'Casey. Dublin has again rocked the cradle of a reputation. From such a theatre as this went forth the fame of Synge. Equally, the fame of O'Casey is born here tonight. This is his apotheosis." (O'Casey afterwards admitted he didn't know if he was being praised or damned until he went home and looked up "apotheosis" in a dictionary.)

Today the Irish theatrical scene is much more mellow here. Actors drop in and out between rehearsals and there's a lot of talk about things literary, as one might expect. Wannabes and have-beens all lock horns within these walls, looking forward to the future or mourning the past – or even soliloquising about what might have been. Whatever their mood, few of them are short of a quotation or two from well-thumbed tomes to illustrate it.

Across the road is an equally unshowy theatrical pub, the Plough. With it's open hearth to warm cold evenings, it's well worth a visit.

# THE PARNELL MOONEY

72 PARNELL STREET

The Parnell Mooney is named after the great Irish political leader and Home Rule activist Charles Stewart Parnell, as indeed is the street in which it's situated. It exudes an air of conviviality and, like its near-neighbour Patrick Conway's, it has in the past lubricated a huge number of fathers-to-be as they waited for news from the Rotunda maternity hospital across the street.

Parnell (1846–91), a Protestant Irishman, was elected to Westminster in 1875 and fought all his short life for the rights of oppressed Catholics. He was hugely popular with one and all, but

**Above** The Parnell Mooney has traditionally helped settle the nerves of expectant fathers

75

support for him fell away after his adulterous relationship with Katherine ("Kitty") O'Shea came to public light.

Kitty was married to Captain William O'Shea when she fell for Parnell in 1880. Two years later she had a child by him. They set up house together and had three children in all, but the scandal cost Parnell the leadership of the Home Rule Party. He was also a highly sensitive man and was emotionally devastated when O'Shea divorced Kitty, citing him as co-respondent. He married her in 1891 and died in her arms four months later, aged just 45.

Most people felt that the strain induced by the scandal (he was also condemned by the clergy) was the most significant factor in the decline of Parnell's health. His funeral, which drew more than 200,000 mourners, was the largest since that of the Liberator Daniel O'Connell in 1847. Parnell's youth was a factor, and there was also a degree of anger about the manner of his passing. Some wreaths even carried the message "Murdered by Priests". In 1911 a statue of Parnell was erected near the pub.

The Rotunda Hospital was founded in 1745 by Bartholomew Mosse, a surgeon who was so disgusted by the horrendous conditions in which the poor gave birth, and the high level of infant mortality, that he devoted himself to raising money for its construction. He also converted the grounds around the hospital and in time these gardens became something of a haven for the aristocracy to visit. In time, the Rotunda Gardens became famous far and wide for their beauty and Mosse used visitors' money to fund the running of the hospital.

Round the corner from the pub is the Garden of Remembrance, which was opened in 1966 to commemorate the 50th anniversary of the Easter Rising of 1916. There's an artificial lake here in cruciform shape and also a sculpture of the folk story "The Children of Lir".

Across the road from this is Belvedere College, where James Joyce was a pupil in the late 1890s. (Much of the material from *A Portrait of the Artist as a Young Man* came out of his experiences here.) The college faces the James Joyce Cultural Centre on North Great Georges Street.

Also nearby is the Gate Theatre, which was founded in 1928 by the actor, painter and writer Micheál Mac Liammóir and his life-long friend Hilton Edwards. The premises they used had also been built by Mosse to raise funds for the hospital. Orson Welles gave his first theatrical performances here as a young man, and James Mason was another thespian ingenue. After "The Boys" (as Edwards and Mac Liammóir were affectionately called) died, Michael Colgan took over the running of the theatre.

A reminder of the area's rustic past is the horse trough near the theatre entrance; if you want another ticket to the past, visit Moore Street, one of Dublin's oldest open-air food markets, and let the colourful traders entertain you with their banter.

The Parnell Mooney, which dates back to 1868 when William Cade was the proprietor, has retained its character well. The central counter is edged with a brass foot-rail, and many arched partitions around it feature stained-glass designs and brass surrounds. Old wooden whiskey barrels protrude from the walls, inscribed with their manufacturers' name. There are mirrored pillars and a wide staircase leads to the upstairs lounge. It's a popular establishment, with discos at the weekend both upstairs and in the basement.

A regular visitor over the years was Brendan Behan, who joined the Irish Republican Army as a young man and spent many years in prison before writing his first play, *The Quare Fellow*, in 1954 and gaining literary celebrity; he was frequently accompanied by his cousin Seamus de Búrca. One day in 1962 Behan said to de Búrca: "The trouble with me is that I should be drinking stout all the time – but since I got well known I can afford spirits". And thereby hangs a tale.

# PATRICK CONWAY'S

70 PARNELL STREET

This was first licensed in 1745, making it the oldest pub in the north of the city. One of Dublin's proudest and most venerable houses, it has remained almost unchanged since its then-owner James Hennessy renovated it back in 1886. Standing on the corner of Moore Lane and Parnell Street, it's generally regarded as a bridgehead between ancient and modern Dublin.

The first proprietor was one John Nixon. After his tenure the pub became known as Doyle's Tavern; then in 1873 it was called Eglinton's. Hennessy took it over in the 1880s and subsequently went on to become Alderman of Dublin (there's a large "H" etched into the stained glass at the entrance to acknowledge him). In the Easter Rising of 1916 the pub was caught up in one of the last, doomed offensives of the nationalists. When they escaped from the General Post Office on O'Connell Street it was Moore Lane they ran to. Here for two days they were splayed with machine-gun fire from the British, who had taken up an unassailable position across the street. Writer and educationist Patrick Pearse, who led the insurgents, was wounded outside the pub and surrendered. A plaque commemorating this event was unveiled outside the bar in 1995 on the pub's 250th anniversary.

The pub was regarded as a masterpiece of mahogany craftsmanship even when it was first designed. The roomy bar has a plush red carpet and a welcoming air. Film buffs might recognise the place from its appearance in the screen adaptation of Roddy Doyle's *The Snapper*, and stills from the film are dotted about the walls.

Above the impressive central counter, made of mahogany, is a precious Anderson clock more than 140 years old. (It's the only one

of its type which is still working.) A multitude of little drawers on the counter betray the pub's origin as a grocery. To underline the point, large mirrors advertise now-defunct products such as Clarke's Famous Dublin Tobacco, Player's Navy Mixture and Goodbody's Famous Irish Roll and Plug. "Family Grocer" reads one of the stained-glass windows.

A sketch shows the pub as it used to look in the early years of the last century. A group of bowler-hatted, walrus-moustachioed men sit astride a counter and table as a rather officious waiter arrives with some dishes. Meanwhile in the corner a docker leans up against a window-sill smoking a pipe and holding a tankard. There's also a portrait of the eponymous Patrick Conway, bespectacled and follically challenged. The story goes that this man was so generous to his barmen, he used to give each of them a penny every Sunday to be put into the collection plate at Mass. Invariably though, they kept the penny to spend on a pint of stout at a rival establishment.

**Above** Patrick Conway's – a 250-year-old masterpiece in mahogany

# NANCY HAND'S

30-32 PARKGATE STREET

This tourist magnet is located just minutes from the Phoenix Park, the largest enclosed urban park in Europe. A wall some eight miles long surround a staggering 1752 acres – in fact, it's bigger than the combined areas of London's Hyde Park, Kensington Gardens, Regent's Park, St James' Park, Green Park and Hampstead Heath. Hardly surprising, then, that more than 235 species of wild animals and tropical birds roam round the enclosed spaces here. Most of them are in the zoo, opened in 1831 and the third oldest in the world (only London and Paris pre-date it). The MGM lion was reared here, and the zoo is also famous for breeding endangered species. The park's name (always prefixed by the definite article, for some unknown reason) isn't an allusion to the mythical bird but is a direct translation of the Gaelic *fionn uisce* (pronounced "fin ishke") which means "clear water" and refers to the spring in the zoo.

Originally priory land, it became a royal deer park in 1671 and finally became a public space in 1747. Deer are still visible on occasion. In the park today are heritage trails, ornamental gardens, more than 40 soccer pitches and a huge training ground for cricket, gaelic football, hurling and *camogie* (a kind of hurling for women).There's a plethora of interesting monuments, and a huge array of plant life and trees, including oak, chestnut and fir hawthorn. The place usually buzzes with activity and there's a steady stream of motorists, cyclists, joggers and pedestrians. It is also a venue to occasional concerts.

The Garda headquarters is in the park, in a building constructed for the Royal Irish Constabulary between 1839 and 1842. Also here is

**Right** Nancy Hand's copper frieze frontage was plundered from a Welsh butcher's shop

**Above and right** Nancy Hand's is a lovingly assembled shrine to the joys of Victoriana

Áras an Uachtaráin, the official residence of the Irish president, built
in 1751, and nearby are the residences of the papal nuncio and the US
ambassador. In 1882 Lord Frederick Cavendish, the British chief
secretary to Ireland, and his under-secretary Thomas Burke were
assassinated opposite the Áras by members of a nationalist group
called The Invincibles.

The current president is Mary McAleese. Her status is somewhat overshadowed by the great achievements of her predecessor, Mary Robinson, who revolutionised the role of president, changing it from that of somebody who shook hands with foreign dignitaries to one who could effect real changes at a political level. Robinson also started the practice of putting a candle in the window for those from Ireland's "fifth province". There are only four geographical provinces in the country; the fifth province refers metaphorically to travellers and emigrants — or, more generally, any restless or homeless souls.

Nancy Hand's is the ultimate theme bar, awash with Victoriana. Proprietor PJ McCaffrey appears to have plundered half of the British Isles to build it stone by stone, using antique fixtures and fittings from a multiplicity of sources, not all of them obvious. The seats are made from the pew of a Yorkshire church; the staircase comes from Trinity College, Dublin (it featured in the film *Educating Rita*), the copper frieze frontage from a butcher's shop in Wales.

Antique bottles abound, as do precious Guinness memorabilia. There's a huge open hearth, and at the top of the stairs a clock embedded into a harp with a little tower on each side. This also was retrieved from a demolished building. Almost every inch of wall space carries a painting of some description. There's a huge steel chandelier hanging from the domed ceiling, and various lanterns elsewhere.

Other curiosities include a postage-stamp dispenser inside the door, and an old postbox across from it. There are crests and plants, candelabra and cabinets, jugs, statues and whatnot scattered pell-mell in the vast split-level interior.

Only part of the building had been a pub before (the Deer Park) but in 1996 McCaffrey bought the surrounding premises to help fashion his little empire. He does a huge food trade as well, both in the restaurant and the carvery bar. The variety of food and drink available is impressive, with over two hundred different brands of whiskey.

**Left** The pub's staircase was pilfered from the hallowed halls of Trinity College

# RYAN'S OF PARKGATE STREET

28 PARKGATE STREET

Even hardened cynics find it difficult to say anything negative about this beautifully preserved watering-hole, which thinks enough of itself to make that careful distinction in its moniker from the many other Ryan's pubs in Dublin.

The present tavern was built and licensed in the 1840s. It's not showy, but you can't fail to be captivated by its carved oak and mahogany central bar, the self-contained snug at the front through which the barman passes your drinks and the antique engraved mirrors. There's a preservation order on the outside of the building, but whatever has remained inside — or been restored — is down to the discernment and initiative of its long line of owners. Peter Farrell, the present proprietor, continues the tradition: his concern for Victoriana is evident in every detail, from the huge pair of gas lamps to the tiny brass match-lighters that are fixed to the counter. The large mechanical clock (wound by key), which goes right across the top of the counter from one side of the bar to the other, is said to be the oldest double-faced centrepiece in any Irish pub.

Sepia photographs on the walls evoke scenes from the past: a boat race in Killiney in 1902, a horse-racing scene in the marina at Cork in 1896, and Dublin's College Green in 1923, when trams were still in use. Perhaps the most interesting is that of a woman in a headscarf peeling potatoes into an old cooking pot as her husband sits across the room from her in a bowler hat, his legs crossed as he reads a letter. Neither of them seem vaguely interested in communicating with one another. It perfectly portrays the dismal, grinding poverty that was once part of everyday life for the working classes.

**Left** Ryan's wonderfully sober Victorian frontage has a preservation order on it

Also treasurable are the little snugs on each side of the counter, two throw-backs to a time when the main areas of bars were "men only" preserves and women retired here to imbibe. Today such snugs are open to anyone, of course – and bookable: in the recent past they've been used by the likes of pop band U2, the French ambassador and various other VIPs anxious for some privacy in an otherwise vibrant atmosphere.

The pub's proximity to Heuston Station guarantees it huge crowds whenever there's an international sporting event, with droves of supporters for the Irish soccer/Gaelic/rugby teams piling in from the trains for liquid refreshment. Another time the pub is heaving is on St Patrick's Day. According to the manager Dave Mullen, in 1999 no fewer than 14 US radio stations phoned on this day to create live links with the large number of Irish expatriates in states such as New York and Massachusetts. He recalls that beads of sweat broke out on his forehead as he tried to serve an innumerable amount of people warbling "Danny Boy" out of tune for the delectation of the shillelagh-and-shamrock brigade across the pond.

Upstairs is Ryan's celebrated restaurant, winner of several awards for its fine cuisine. It's long, narrow and intimate, the abstract art on the walls the only evidence of modernity. At each end there's an open fireplace with mahogany surrounds, rounding off the old world feel. (The "turf fires" are actually gas-lit, as otherwise the insurance would be prohibitive.)

The whole place is like a little world of its own, a window onto the past. In the 1980s, when there seemed to be big money to be made by modernising pubs (which usually meant sanitising them), it kept its Victorian integrity, and it is now regarded as something of an oasis in a desert of superpub mediocrity. Simplicity, sometimes, is the hallmark of genius.

**Above** Ryan's elegant carved and mirrored Victorian mahogany partitions

## ST STEPHEN'S GREEN

# DAVY BYRNE'S

21 DUKE STREET

J ames Joyce would probably turn in his grave if he saw what they've done to his old haunt. The main refurbishment took place in 1941, the year he died, but he had made his home on foreign shores long before that time.

He immortalised Davy Byrne's as a "moral" pub in *Ulysses*, presumably because it forbade gambling. Now, every 16 June – the day on which the whole of that book is set, being the day Joyce met his muse Nora Barnacle – vast numbers of "Bloomsday" buffs descend upon the place and order the meal Leopold Bloom had here on that day: a gorgonzola cheese sandwich with mustard, and a glass of burgundy on the side. They dress in period costume as well, and there are innumerable walks and talks; but Davy Byrne's is the focus of the annual madness, largely engineered by people who confess to having struggled unsuccessfully with the more obscure passages of the book. Of course it's mainly an excuse for a booze-up, and Irish people love these. The fact that while imbibing one can trade quips and epigrams – if not quite reach illuminatory epiphanies – is the icing on the cake.

Other literary patrons have included Brendan Behan and the poet Pádraic Ó Conaire. The latter used to tether his donkey and cart to a lamp-post while inside. (Today's patron is more likely to be driving a BMW.) Behan and JP Donleavy had a dust-up here once, Behan

**Right** Davy Byrne's – a pub made legend, thanks to James Joyce

insulting Donleavy and Donleavy asking him outside as a result. As they got ready to fight, Behan suddenly put his arm round Donleavy and said, "Why should the pair of us beat the bejesus out of each other for the satisfaction of eejits like them inside who wouldn't know a present participle from a hole in their buried mothers' coffins?" Donleavy agreed, so instead of squaring up to each other

**Above** The early 1940s interior at Davy Byrne's has an art-deco feel to it

they went for a drink elsewhere. Asked to explain why they had no bruises afterwards, Behan replied, "We were so fast getting out of each other's way, neither of us could land a punch".

In the early 1900s, Sinn Féin leader Michael Collins attended cabinet meetings upstairs. In fact during the Anglo-Irish Treaty negotiations he's reputed to have sent a telegram to the pub asking Byrne to post him over a brandy "to settle the vexed Irish question". (Every time it was settled, David Lloyd George once quipped, "the Irish changed the question!") On the night the treaty was signed, Arthur Griffith and members of the Executive Council of the Irish Free State toasted the success of the negotiations on these same premises.

The current proprietor is Redmond Doran, the third generation of Dorans to have owned it. Proudly displayed is the "Bloom's Bell", presented to the pub in 1991 by local antiquarians in honour of its centenary (a little late, but never mind). It bears the inscription: "Lest we forget all who pass through here, time be damned."

The main bar has an impressive ceiling, with leaf and fruit designs indented into it. There are also two chandeliers with tulip lights. There's a white marble counter which has been strengthened by hundreds of wine bottle bottoms cemented together under it. You will also see a swan mural, a copper mural of Joyce, a sculpture in the shape of a beehive, and ten mirrors in the back lounge. Forking off the lounge is a third bar, The Arcade.

There are so many literary echoes here, Flann O'Brien wrote: "The premises bear openly the marks of their departed guests, like traces of fresh stout from in a glass by a policeman after hours". The modern Davy Byrne's is an up-beat, up-market establishment that has a busy food trade as well, with seafood a speciality – after the burgundy, of course, and the gorgonzola cheese.

# THE DUKE

9 DUKE STREET

Named after the second Duke of Grafton, Lord Lieutenant to Ireland from 1721 to 1723, the Duke was established in 1822. It was refurbished some years ago in the ornate style of early Georgian Dublin, which resulted in a large increase in its patronage. The new custom has sometimes been accused of being "posey", but it's a very agreeable place to have a bite and a sup, with lots of nooks and crannies. There are any number of wall sketches, most notably a huge collage of all the usual literary suspects: Yeats, Kavanagh, Flann O'Brien and so on. An impressive staircase with murals on the wall leads you to an equally attractive bar upstairs.

In a little hideaway are some fascinating framed letters from James Joyce. One of them, sent to Harriet Shaw Weaver from Paris in 1926, has him getting demonstrably excited about the fact that "Gens de Dublin" (*Dubliners*) has gone into its eighth edition. He also confides that he once threw away the original manuscript of *Ulysses* in a fit of pique resulting from "the trouble" over that book, but the "charred remains" were rescued by "a family fire brigade".

There's also a letter to TS Eliot on New Year's Day 1932, in which Joyce tells him of the death of his father. He feels guilt over the fact that he never returned to Ireland to see him, despite repeated reassurances that he would, but says he had developed very negative feelings towards the country for a number of reasons. One of these was the banning of *Dubliners* (on the advice of a person he thought was a friend). Joyce adds that his wife Nora paid a visit home during the Civil War in 1922 and was almost killed in a hail of bullets on a train one day. She lay flat on the floor of the railway carriage while rival

parties shot at each other above her head.

In another letter, sent from Trieste in Italy in 1920 to his aunt, Mrs William Murray, Joyce importunes her for details about Dublin (Had the Star of the Sea Church ivy on its seafront? Were the trees in Leahy's Terrace at the side or rear?) so that he can finalise two chapters of *Ulysses*. He ends by telling her — apparently with some delight — that

**Above** The Duke, established in 1822

the American censor burned all the copies of the last issue of the *Little Review* because it featured an extract from *Ulysses.*

The pub is situated next door to Cathach Books which specialises in rare Irish publications, so it's a fitting place for the Jameson Literary Pubcrawl to begin. Tours are conducted by professional actors, who take groups to a selection of Dublin's best-known literary pubs and give readings of the works of Joyce, Brendan Behan and Samuel Beckett, among others. It's a kind of walkabout seminar that frees literature from the aridity of academia. It's irreverent and great fun, and an indirect way of seeing pubs one might not otherwise be aware of. Tours takes place every night from Easter until the end of October, and occasional evenings in winter.

Pedestrianised Grafton Street and its shops are nearby. You may see buskers playing music here and be tempted to place a coin in their hat, or perhaps drop into the world famous Bewley's for tea or coffee. There are three branches of Bewley's in Dublin (the other two being in Westmoreland Street and South Great Georges Street) but this is the original. It's been a traditional haven for everybody from fatigued shoppers to shaggy-haired students. Time was that you could linger here over your drink forever and a day without anybody being aware of your presence, but lately there's been a system whereby a waitress leads patrons to their seats to order.

Also nearby is Leinster House, the seat of the *Dáil,* or Irish Parliament, in Kildare Street. This was built by Richard Castle in the mid 1700s and now houses offices and debating chambers for 166 members of parliament, or TDs (from the Gaelic *teachtaí dálaí*).

The Mansion House is situated on Dawson Street, which is also within walking distance. A Queen Anne-style residence that dates from 1705 (the stucco and wrought iron exterior was added later), it has been the home of Lord Mayors of Dublin since 1715.

**Left** The Duke's stairway renovated in Georgian style

# THE BAILEY

2–3 DUKE STREET

I t's hard to tell now from the modern exterior and décor, but the Bailey has a long history. It started life as an eating-house in 1837. Nicholas Bailey bought the premises in 1856, and the pub carries his name to this day. It was a favourite bolthole of Arthur Griffith, the founder of Sinn Féin and later president of the Irish Free State in 1922. Rebel leader Michael Collins used to risk drinking here when he was on the run from the British Army, even as members of the dreaded Black and Tans militias were imbibing on the same premises downstairs.

The bar was wholly behind the rebels: if a stranger entered when republicans were engaging in discussion, the barman would always

**Above and right** The Bailey's modern facade and interior hide a wealth of history

signal by a gesture – a flick of the hand, a nod of the head, a brush of the shoulder – to let them know there was a potential undercover agent in the camp. Many Black and Tans walked into traps when they raided bars that were known to be dens of rebel activity. These "safe houses" were often forewarned of their visits by their spies at Dublin Castle. But if they arrived unexpectedly, IRA men often found

themselves in the position of having to eat little bits of paper with secret messages on them for fear of being captured and exposed.

The first proponent of Home Rule in the Victorian era, statesman Isaac Butt, drank here, as did members of the United Irishmen and the Irish Republican Brotherhood. It's said that Charles Stewart Parnell, whose political career was destroyed by his love for the already-married Kitty O'Shea, appeared publicly with her for the last time in the upstairs dining-room in 1891.

In the 1880s Bailey's was owned by one James Joyce – not the author, one hastens to add, but the place was to make its mark in literary history. It was more a restaurant than a bar when John Ryan (the late broadcaster, publisher, writer and set designer) bought it for a

knockdown price in 1958, and he made it his ambition to restore its original character. This he did, and in doing so made it the favoured stomping-ground of many of Dublin's famous literary figures such as Flann O'Brien, Oliver St John Gogarty and JP Donleavy. In many ways it was the Dublin equivalent of New York's Algonquin Hotel, a home-from-home for the era's Bright Young Things. One wag emoted that the Bailey drinkers would "sacrifice their mothers for a witty phrase".

James Joyce also used to drink here, and even though he doesn't mention the pub in *Ulysses*, until recently the Bailey used to display the door of Leopold Bloom's house – 7 Eccles Street, now part of the Mater Hospital. In 1967 Ryan saved it from wreckers when the original property, owned by Joyce's friend John Francis Byrne (who features as Cranly in *A Portrait of the Artist as a Young Man*), was knocked down; it was proudly unveiled on "Bloomsday", 16 June. The door is now housed at the James Joyce Cultural Centre.

Brendan Behan was also a patron; in fact he claimed to have "bought" the Bailey by accident one day in 1955 when he was drunk and found himself bidding for it at an auction when all he had meant to buy was an electric toaster. He was thrown out of here many times, as he was from most pubs he frequented. Patrick Kavanagh was also asked to leave once, because he refused to remove his hat. He always claimed he felt undressed without it on his head. International figures who sought out the Bailey while on trips to Dublin include Charlie Chaplin and Evelyn Waugh.

Ryan was forced to demolish most of the building in the mid 1960s after pressure was brought to bear on him by the Dublin Corporation Dangerous Buildings Section. It broke his heart to have to do this, but so admired was he by this time, that he still didn't lose the custom of the literati. He eventually sold up in 1971 and from then onwards the anecdotal merriment of the place diminished rapidly.

The marble counter is gone, as is the sense of history, the decor at present having a contemporary theme. Marks & Spencer is also next door now, which further underlines the bland, business-like ethos. Such an ethos attracts the monied set more than struggling scribes, or the tellers of colourful tales about Ireland's literary and republican past, but while you're here, why not toast the times past?

# KEHOE'S

9 ANNE STREET SOUTH

This very popular pub was first licensed in 1803 and has changed little since the Victorian era, carrying its age with understated elegance. The electric light fittings are about the newest items on view, and these date back at least 70 years. As you look at the smoke-stained walls here and savour the ambience, it's like taking a time capsule into Dublin's magic past.

It was once a grocery, as you'll gather from the ads for such items as Bendigo Plug Tobacco or Teddy Chocolate, and the 28 mahogany drawers on your left as you enter the saloon-style door. They once used to contain rice, tea and snuffs, which customers would order on their way towards liquid replenishment in the back bar. Sitting amid the tastefully carved mahogany is a rickety old whiskey churner hanging rakishly from the wall, an ornamental reminder of when the former proprietor John Kehoe used to make his own whiskey on the premises.

There are many snugs, separated by wooden partitions. In one of them there's a buzzer and a serving hatch: rarities in any pub today. Another one used to be the ladies' loo. The current toilet is reached by a door so low you're warned to watch your head as you pass through. Many's the time the likes of Flann O'Brien, Patrick Kavanagh and Brendan Behan hit their skulls here, but were too drunk to feel the pain. (The writers used to repair to Kehoe's when their jubilant antics proved too much for the proprietor and/or customers of nearby McDaid's.)

Other curious items are a turn-of-the-century till and a huge fridge behind the counter, making you wonder if you've had one too many and have suddenly arrived back in your kitchen. John Kehoe

used to live upstairs, but since his death these quarters have become part of the bar itself.

Kehoe's is a relaxed place, and the sartorially elegant are sometimes said to "dress down" before they come in here so they can fraternise more comfortably with their rough-and-ready counterparts. Much admired for the manner in which it's changed so little over the years, the pub has become a popular pit-stop for those who've just visited one of the many art galleries in the area. Here you may also find yourself buttonholed by a man who knows the solution to all the country's problems. If so, humour him: the decor demands it. There are a lot worse places to have to suffer bores.

**Above** Kehoe's, where little seems to have changed in the past hundred years

# McDAID'S

3 HARRY STREET

McDaid's may not have quite as much bohemian character as it possessed in the 1950s, when literary drinkers like Patrick Kavanagh and Brendan Behan held court here, but equally it hasn't sold out to sanitisation like so many of its ilk. With a prime location just a stone's throw away from Grafton Street, it's as beloved of true-blue Dubliners as it is of transient tourists anxious to grab a slice of Dublin in the "rare oul' times".

The building, which dates from 1873, was originally Dublin's morgue, and it also became a chapel for the Moravian brethren, who developed the practice of standing corpses in a vertical position. (This is said to be the main reason for the pub's high ceilings.) In the early 1900s it was a hive of republican activity, and many of its patrons then included men recently released from internment camps in England, which resulted in a strong presence of British undercover Special Branch detectives around the time of the Easter Rising of 1916.

Many actors also dropped in for their pre- and post-performance libations. Dramatic stalwarts Noel Purcell and Jimmy O'Dea drank here in their time, as did Gainor Crist, the inspiration behind Sebastian Dangerfield in JP Donleavy's *The Ginger Man*. Other writers who frequented it include Liam O'Flaherty, Austin Clarke, Tony Cronin and John Jordan.

Tales of manic nights here are legendary in Irish pub lore. Poteen, the (in)famous Irish high-proof, moonshine spirit, is alleged to have been dispensed regularly with a nudge and a wink.

McDaid's retains much of its appeal, and fledgling scribes like to soak up the literary atmosphere still in evidence. Brendan Behan

actually took over a corner of the bar here in the 1950s, arriving with his battered typewriter one day and writing as he drank – often to *pay* for that drink. He also offered to paint the McDaid's toilet on occasion for the price of a few pints. (He was, of course, a house-painter by trade.) Yeats could have his castle and Joyce his tower, he roared; he had his little province at that table. There's a photo of him sitting at it with two pint glasses beside him, one full and one empty, as he types, a cigarette hanging from his lips.

In the 1930s it was almost entirely a working-class pub. It was also rather dowdy and run-down, but in the latter part of the decade, writer John Ryan, the editor of the literary magazine *Envoy*, practically used it as his office. He gathered around him many writers and gave them work, edited their material – often on the premises – and officiated between them during disputes, which were manifold.

**Above** McDaid's – once a mecca for Dublin's literary imbibers

According to barman Paddy O'Brien he was the "founder member" of McDaid's Mark Two, and the pub became the "in" place largely due to his influence, as he drew the literati like a magnet.

Paddy was barman here from 1937 to 1972 and described it as a place of sawdust and spitoons, where elderly men in little groups spent most of their time spitting on the floor or into the spitoons, which he had to clean out every morning. At a time when tuberculosis was rampant, this was a task he undertook with not a little nervousness.

There was no forelock-tugging, no obsequiousness to "the writer". On the other hand, people who came in to rabbit on about football or women — the classic pub-talk fodder — were bewildered to discover that they were in the minority. Tony Cronin claims it was never a literary pub *per se*; that its attraction was its chameleon nature. "The division between writer and non-writer," he wrote in *Dead as Doornails*, "was never rigorously enforced. Neither was the distinction between

**Above** Before it was a pub, McDaid's had been both a morgue and a chapel

informer or revolutionary". No matter which side of the socio-political divide you inhabited, no questions were asked. It was just a melting-pot. It was also once described as a haven for "university professors who drank too much, and visiting US millionairesses".

Paddy used to wonder how Kavanagh, Behan and Flann O'Brien — who all died of alcohol-related conditions in the 1960s — could manage to drink so much and still function as writers. Kavanagh and Behan could at least set their own schedules, but O'Brien was holding down a journalistic post at the *Irish Times* (writing under the pseudonym Myles na Gopaleen) and had to file copy every day, not an easy task when he was almost always blotto by mid-afternoon. Paddy concluded that he must have gone home to sleep each evening and set the clock for a dawn writing session.

Behan was an equally pathetic prospect in Paddy's eyes. He remembered him falling asleep from drink in the pub even from the tender age of 17, a curly-haired, windswept tearaway with his shirt hanging out and his eyes wide with devilment. Kavanagh was his usual foil, but he would pick a fight with anyone just for the hell of it. Paddy threw him out many times for "stirring the pot" but always allowed him back the following day. He didn't believe in barring people because he felt it created bad blood. Besides, he enjoyed the banter too much.

Behan could never hold his drink, Paddy claimed. He got drunk very quickly and after that you were looking at trouble with a capital T. It was usually Kavanagh that was on the receiving end of his bile because he knew Kavanagh was afraid of him and he played on that. When a satire of Kavanagh appeared in a magazine in the 1960s, Kavanagh believed Behan had written it and sued the magazine for defamation of character, but lost the case. He later developed cancer. Many felt the stress of the case destroyed his health — and ultimately his life.

# NEARY'S

## 1 CHATHAM STREET

This has a prime location near Stephen's Green, a place popular with city centre workers who go to unwind among its sheltered paths. Dublin, as the song says, can be heaven, with coffee at eleven, and a stroll through Stephen's Green.

The Green was formerly an open common. It was enclosed in 1663, but not surrounded by buildings until the late 18th century, and became a public park in 1880 after the Guinness family invested money in its development. It contains a Victorian bandstand which is sometimes used for concerts, a hump-backed bridge, a beautiful array of flower beds and an artificial lake which, in the evocative phrase of novelist and poet George Moore, "curves like a piece of calligraphy". Several statues commemorate some of Ireland's greatest sons: 18th-century nationalists Wolfe Tone and Robert Emmet, Thomas Kettle, the poet who died in World War I, and James Joyce. On the south side of the Green is Iveagh House, where the Guinness family lived for a time. It is now the Department of Foreign Affairs.

The west side used to be where executions took place, a gibbet occupying the place where the Royal College of Surgeons now stands. This much admired classical building was one of the rebel strongholds during the Easter Rising of 1916. (There are still chips in the stonework from the bullets.) When Countess Markievicz, a society beauty who joined the rebels, found herself in charge here, the first question she asked was "Where are the scalpels?" – she wanted to use them as bayonets. Two years later she was elected Sinn Fein MP – Britain's first woman MP – but refused to take her seat at Westminster because she would have had to swear allegiance to the King.

**Right** Neary's with its famous lamp-holding sentinel bronze arms

Also on the Green is Newman House, which originally housed University College. The English theologian and Catholic convert John Henry Newman was a rector here; poet and fellow convert Gerard Manley Hopkins a former professor of Classics. James Joyce, nationalist Patrick Pearse and statesman Éamon de Valera attended it. The building (designed by Richard Cassell who is also responsible for the seat of government, Leinster House) dates from 1740 and is decorated with rococo plasterwork and marble-tiled floors and is one of the finest Georgian buildings in the city.

Neary's (also sometimes called the Chatham Lounge) exudes an air of sumptuous old-world opulence. You could hardly miss it – its brick and limestone frontage is marked by two black sculpted bronze arms, holding lighted globes aloft. Inside, it has a strong Edwardian feel about it, with its plush red carpet, mirrored wall at the back and ornate brass fittings. The bar counter is marble-topped, with mahogany surrounds. There's a smaller bar to the left of the entrance, and another one upstairs.

The pub backs onto the Gaiety Theatre, and many music hall performers in years gone by conquered their nerves here with a "ball of malt" or two before taking to the stage. It's a favourite with Peter O'Toole, who often makes a pit-stop whenever he journeys home between acting engagements overseas. Many Dublin writers have supped here too: Flann O'Brien was a patron, as was Patrick Kavanagh – the latter usually to escape the drunken taunts of Brendan Behan in the nearby McDaid's. The story most associated with Kavanagh from his days in Neary's concerns the time he had his poetry spread out over the counter and a trainee barman spilled a pint over it. Kavanagh looked up at him with his familiar crusty expression and droned, "You may not make much of a barman, son, but you're an effin' brilliant judge of poetry!"

Another Neary's tale recounts how John Ryan (a former owner of the Bailey) was here one time with the partially-sighted British poet John Heath-Stubbs when he decided to go to a bookie's office down the road to put a bet on a horse. Heath-Stubbs tagged behind him a little worse for wear. When they got to the bookie's he thought they had entered another bar and made his way to the "counter", calling for a fresh round of drinks for everyone.

Many Dublin pubs count celebrities among their customers, but here they even claim a past owner as a celebrity. Leo Neary, the propreitor after whom the pub is named, eventually went on to become the Honorary Consul to the Republic of Guatemala.

**Above** Inside, Neary's still has a mood of Edwardian old-world charm

# SHELBOURNE HOTEL

27 ST STEPHEN'S GREEN

A classic stop-over for the blue-chip fraternity, the Shelbourne is something of an institution in Irish life. It was originally the town house of Thomas Fitzmaurice, the First Earl of Kerry. After he died in 1590 it passed to his son, the First Earl of Shelbourne, and then to another son, also called Thomas. After his death the house was leased to the army as a troop billet. In 1818, however, one of the soldiers accidentally started a fire and the building burned down. It was then rebuilt and leased to Martin Burke, who turned it into a hotel.

After Burke's death in 1863, it was revamped and opened with such added attractions as a ladies coffee-room, a smoking room, a hairdressing salon, a reading room and a telegraph office. It was extended again in 1886. In the 1870s and 1880s it served as the starting-point for coaches to Bray and Greystones, an added boon to custom. It was one of the first buildings to be provided with electricity after it became available in 1892. The Jury family held control of it until 1960, when it was sold to the Forte Group; Granada took it over in 1996. It still carries an easy sense of Edwardian elegance – the Shelbourne is the kind of hotel where the porters might be expected to see themselves on a higher echelon than the managing director of a small inner city firm.

In 1916, as tea was being served to punters from the Fairyhouse Races, the building shook from the ricochet of bullets fired by Irish rebels in a war most of them probably didn't even know was taking place. They were hemmed in by the revolutionaries on one side and British forces on the other, and wounded bodies were dragged into the hotel, spilling blood over the ornate cutlery. Only a few years later, the

Constitution of the Irish Free State was drafted here.

Many writers have drunk in the Shelbourne, including William Thackeray, Rudyard Kipling and Elizabeth Bowen – who conducted her affair with Sean O'Faoláin here. George Moore set his play *A Drama in Muslin* here, and Graham Greene wrote part of *The End of the Affair* on the premises.

Thackeray had bed and board here in 1821 for six shillings and eight pence a day, which he was quite happy with. Today you would be lucky to get a packet of peanuts for that. Oliver St John Gogarty also stayed here, from 1915 to 1917. James Cagney danced on the piano, and John F Kennedy paid a visit with his wife Jacqueline in 1958 when he was campaigning for the US presidential nomination. Past Hollywood guests include Rock Hudson, Montgomery Clift and John Huston. Peter O'Toole took a room here when he was appearing in *Waiting for Godot* in the Abbey Theatre in the early 1970s; legend has it

**Above** The Shelbourne was originally the town house of the First Earl of Kerry

he took a bath one night in a tub filled with (what else?) 24 magnums of champagne. Princess Grace was a favourite guest, and the hotel's main suite is named in her honour.

More controversially, in 1943 the Shelbourne was the base for an American spy called Martin S Quigley who passed himself off as a film industry official. He was in fact here to investigate the nature of Ireland's neutrality during World War II. He was entertained by president Éamon de Valera and other heads of state during his sojourn. And let's not forget that, in the years before World War I, Alois Hitler, the Fuhrer's half-brother, worked here as a wine waiter. He went on to marry an Irish girl called Bridget Dowling, who eloped with him to London. He introduced her to Adolf in Liverpool in 1912, and then abandoned her.

You don't have to be staying at the Shelbourne to drop in. The front of the building has changed very little with the years, though there have been a series of overhauls inside. The art deco Egyptian lamp-holders outside prepare you for the opulence of the (fake) marble entrance hall and the chandeliered lobby. Immediately to the right is the Lord Mayor's Lounge, famed for its afternoon tea.

Behind it is the Horseshoe Bar, which dates back to 1857 and holds

**Above and right** The Shelbourne's celebrated Horseshoe Bar built in 1857

a special place in the affections of all
Dubliners. The movers and shakers of
Irish society have always convened
here to exchange tittle-tattle about
who's in and who's out, and what way
governmental opinion is likely to go
on current affairs.

Indeed, it has often been suggested
that the substantive decisions
affecting the country are made here
rather than in the government
buildings down the road. Whether
this is true or not, one imagines a fair
share of deals have been done here
with a nudge and a wink, for this is
where issues are discussed without
anybody having to worry about
television cameras or role-playing.
Barman Sean Boyd calls it "the most
exclusive club in Dublin, and one
which has open membership for all."
It's also the preserve of political
correspondents, media worthies,
gossip columnists and other quotable notables.

Across from the Horseshoe Bar is the newer Shelbourne Bar,
established in 1991. It's an imposing addition that doesn't take itself
too seriously, as one may glean from the satirical sketches of Martyn
Turner on the walls. This is especially packed during the Dublin Horse
Show, or when there are rugby or soccer internationals being played in
Lansdowne Road.

# O'DONOGHUE'S

## 15 MERRION ROW

The *craic* is mighty here at night-time. Everybody knows exactly what to expect from O'Donoghue's, and they usually get it: frivolity is the name of the game, with a little bit of insanity thrown in for good measure. It might not be the first port of call for fastidious drinkers, particularly those who dislike music and hippy traveller types, but there's no gainsaying its raucous energy and life-affirming earthiness.

"There it stands in Merrion Row," reads a piece of doggerel proudly displayed on the pub's wall, "a monument to one and all. They come from Cork and Kerry, County Clare and Donegal." The poem goes on to say that patrons can be assured of receiving stout "as black as a raven's wing" as a fiddler tunes up and the other drinkers tap their feet and clap their hands in appreciation. It finishes up:

*They may talk of foreign lands*
*of France and Palestine*
*of cocktail bars in Malabar*
*or sweet schnapps on the Rhine.*
*They can have their fancy drinks*
*but when it comes to booze*
*you'll never beat the friends you meet*
*in brave O'Donoghue's.*

The pub – or rather the building in which it now stands – was built in 1789. It was originally the property of a family grocer-cum-wine and-spirit-merchant and then passed into the hands of a soldier.

**Right** O'Donoghue's has had a reputation for traditional music since the 1930s

He sold it to the Right Honourable Captain George Vaughn in 1837. The following year it was sold to Christopher Reedy, a saddler. Thirteen years later it was licensed to Timothy Malone along with the property next door. In the following decade the premises was turned into a billiard room, and after that a boot and shoe manufacturing firm. It later became a bar/grocery again under Tom Kennedy, who was the proprietor until 1904, at which time it became a bar pure and simple.

The year 1934 saw the first appearance of the name O'Donoghue outside and the music inside. Dessie Hynes of Longford took it over in 1977 and carried on the music tradition. In 1985 it was gutted by fire, but after extensive repairs and improvements it reopened with a new Liscannor stone floor and central heating to boot.

It won a Guinness Certificate of Excellence in 1994 for its beer quality and strives to maintain these standards. More famously, it gave us The Dubliners. One of the first bars to pick up on the ballad boom of the 1960s, it was here the bearded quartet honed their art, Luke Kelly popularising the songs of Ewan McColl, a lifelong activist for social causes, and Ronnie Drew and the rest lending able support as they improvised sessions at all hours of the day and night to the delight of

**Above** A lunchtime session in full flow at O'Donoghue's

their bewildered auditors.

The first thing you notice is that the walls are covered, mosaic-fashion, with photographs of people who've drunk here in the past. The lion's share of these, it must be said, are musicians, and the lion's share of the musicians are The Dubliners. As well as having a whole wall devoted to them, there are also huge sketches of them, and other snaps of them in action in the back bar, though a cross-section of other celebrities feature here as well. There's a German poster ("Irland's berühmteste folkgruppe") outlining the Dubliners' gigs in that country in the winter of 1976, and their images are even engraved on the huge mirror that adorns the side wall. There are so many photographs and sketches of them on view; in fact, the pub should really be re-named the Ronnie Drew. (Ronnie actually had his wedding reception here. Loyalty doesn't come much greater than that.)

Further photographs, extending even to the beam across the back bar, serve as a kind of social history of the 20th century. There's a shot of the horse-drawn carriage pulling up opposite the pub, another one showing Bertie Ahern getting a guitar lesson from Ronnie in 1987, the group's 25th anniversary.

Christy Moore, Phil Lynott, The Fureys and Paul Brady all practised their trade here in the 1960s, and the evidence is shouting at you. Today you'll still see would-be trad bards striking up a chord or two, even if the folk ballad boom has long gone, and taken the *"bodhrán-and-sleeping-bag"* buffs with it. There's a little courtyard out the back where you can sup your pint on fine days.

Merrion Row, on which the pub sits, was named after the 2nd Viscount Fitzwilliam of Merrion, whose ancestors arrived in Ireland in 1210. Past local residents include WB Yeats (82 Merrion Square), Sheridan Le Fanu (70 Merrion Square) and William Wilde, the father of Oscar, who resided at 1 Merrion Square.

# TONER'S

139 BAGGOT STREET LOWER

This is one of the few pubs in Dublin which has almost totally preserved its true original character. The façade is unadorned Victorian and the floors crooked stone. Originally a spirit grocers, the bar has old-fashioned pump handles, old Irish currency on the walls, a set of dusty books that seem almost pre-Famine, and shelves and drawers that evoke its grocer heritage. You sit on a high stool, survey the neatly-partitioned snugs and feel as if you're in a country pub of a hundred years ago. There's also a cavernous basement bar for good measure – and measures.

Toner's also makes the dubious boast that it's the only pub WB Yeats ever entered. (This is probably untrue, because he seems to have entertained fellow poets in bars in England.) The story goes that one day, not wishing to die wondering how the Irish populace spent their leisure hours, he said to the writer and politician Oliver St John Gogarty, "Do you know, I've never been in a bar in my life." Gogarty immediately set about remedying this state of affairs and commandeered a carriage to take him to this establishment. Yeats entered it with a grimace on his face, and though he lowered a sherry, it didn't do much for him. When his glass was empty, he sat on his stool like a fractious child and said to Gogarty, "I don't like it. Lead me out again." With which, the great man completed his short-lived pub career.

Today's clientele largely consists of a heady brew of "culture vultures" and those with vague connections to the media. The pub makes no attempt to court tourists but they still seek it out, perhaps for that very reason.

A flagship of antiquity, it has a mural of James Joyce and Patrick Kavanagh on the outside wall to prepare you for what you get when you enter. You'll be enthralled by the cosy (if occasionally cliquish) warmth, the lively hum of conversation and the likely prospect of seeing someone from the public eye. Toner's is a spectacular experience of Dublin's everyday past.

**Above and next page** Toner's has preserved its original character with few compromises

# DOHENY & NESBITT'S

5 Baggot Street Lower

Ned Doheny and Tom Nesbitt are two Tipperary men who, after tending bar for a number of years in Dublin, went to America with the express purpose of earning enough money to buy a pub back home. When they returned in 1962, this is the one they chose, and it is now one of the most famous traditional bars in central Dublin. Ned and Tom finally retired in 1990, selling the pub to its current owners Tom and Paul Mangan.

The building is 130 years old, and looks it too, at least judging by the frontage and the main bar. Replete with authentic Victorian fittings, ancient casks and tankards, wooden partitions and stone floors, it's the genuine article. A brass sign on the window notes that

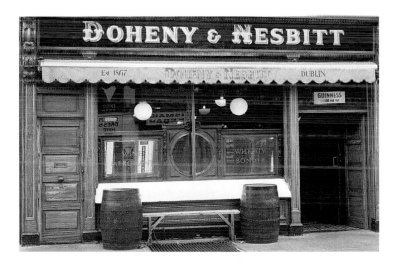

**Above** Doheny & Nesbitt's was, like many a Dublin pub, originally a grocer's shop

it was originally a grocer's shop owned by a tea and wine merchant called John Delahunty. There's a lovely little snug immediately to the right after you enter, a throw-back to the old days when women sat in such places with their glasses of Guinness and the men lined up at the counter. There are glass-panelled partitions in the bar itself, and old posters on the walls.

It enjoyed a moderate trade until the mid-1970s, when things really started to pick up. Nobody is quite sure of the reasons for this, but one theory has it that it all goes back to a very popular barman called Niall Fleming. Fleming originally worked in Madigan's in Donnybrook, which was then the preferred watering-hole of those who worked in RTE, the national radio and television station. (One of the main reasons for his popularity, apparently, was that he cashed the cheques of the RTE staff during a bank strike which almost crippled the country in the 1970s.) In any case, when Fleming moved many drinkers moved with him. In no time at all, the media people were joined by their friends in politics and the civil service, and thus was born a kind of media babble that has come to be known as Nesbittspeak.

Dick Walsh, former political editor of the *Irish Times*, has even coined an acronym to describe the brand of dialogue generally held here. "DANSE" he calls it, which stands for the "Doheny And Nesbitt School of Economics"; the people carrying on such a dialogue are – you've guessed it – Lords of the Danse.

From this point of view, Nesbitt's, as many people call it, has become synonymous with a manner of thinking personified by those who live in Dublin 4, the city's most affluent postal code. It has this quality in common with the Horseshoe Bar (see the Shelbourne). People come here to pontificate, and you can have a good time eavesdropping on some self-satisfied prognostications.

**Left** Traditional wooden partitions at Doheny and Nesbitt's

Oh to have been a fly on the wall here over the years, listening to tales of politicians about to make it big or be deposed, or the inside story on somebody you thought you knew. The stories always broke here first, the ones that would be headlining tomorrow's papers, the scandals and the scoops, trotted out by pressmen who had their tongues loosened by one too many glasses of Guinness.

Octagenarian novelist Ben Kiely likes to tell the story of an initiation rite that tipplers of his era had to undergo in order to prove themselves worthy of being here. It involved drinking 17 pints in quick succession and then buying drinks for everyone in the pub. Apparently, this was one test Brendan Behan passed with flying colours.

Many government departments are situated round the corner on Merrion Street, and unsurpisingly the main clientele here are journalists and politicians, along with "legal eagles" and those from the world of the media in general. Upstairs, carvery lunches are served to people who may well be blissfully unaware of the robust debates taking place on the floor beneath them.

It is said that every man is a king on his barstool, and this watering-hole has them aplenty: raconteurs hungry for laughter, pencil-pushers anxious to hit back at a system they despise, trendy young things anxious to rub shoulders with antiquity – if only for an evening. It is also said that all the people who really know how to run the country, are either driving taxis or cutting people's hair. Not so. Some of them are propping up the counter at Doheny & Nesbitt's.

# THE BLEEDING HORSE

24 UPPER CAMDEN STREET

"There stood at the southern extremity of the city, near the point at which Camden Street now terminates, a small, old-fashioned building, something between an alehouse and an inn". Thus wrote former patron Sheridan Le Fanu about the Bleeding Horse in his historical novel *The Cock and the Anchor* in 1845, and his impressions still hold true today.

Once a halting spot for coachmen who needed to re-shoe horses, it's one of the most picturesque and well-preserved of Dublin's pubs. The present commanding structure dates from 1710.

Inside, it has the air of an ancient coaching house with its serpentine nooks and crannies, which wind through both of its impressive floors.

**Above** The Bleeding Horse – the closest thing to a coaching house in the city centre

BLEEDING HORSE
T-SHIRT
£8.00

BEWARE
PICKPOCKETS
AND
LOOSE WOMEN

There's a first-floor gallery edged with wooden railings that once graced a church looking down on the main floor of the pub and the plethora of exposed beams in the central space emphasise its lofty grandeur.

Upstairs, in glass cases, are more testaments to the ordinary business of previous times, such as a receipt from the 1940s for a set of weighing scales. Pictures of writers connected to the pub include that of JP Donleavy, who mentions it in his first novel, *The Ginger Man*. Sheridan Le Fanu, whose portrait is also here, is widely believed to have helped Bram Stoker work on his novel, *Dracula*, within these very walls. It was one of James Joyce's favourite watering-holes, and it features in *Ulysses*, his seminal "stream-of-consciousness" novel about events in a single Dublin day. It is said that Joyce was thrown out of here one night when he was caught looking up the skirt of an actress after falling down the stairs drunk.

The pub has also been the site of much secret plotting: the United Irishmen who agitated against British rule in the 1790s frequently met here, as did their political brothers the Fenians in the late 19th and early 20th century.

There are two theories as to the origin of the adjective in the pub's name. One suggests that it results from the former habit of surgically draining fluid from behind the ears of horses who were suffering from shaking fits after arduous journeys. Another claims that after Oliver Cromwell's army defeated the Royalists here in 1649, he had his "bleeding" steeds treated on the premises. It was briefly called the Falcon at one time, because a previous owner felt the titular adjective was vulgar. (In Dublin parlance, it has the same ambiguity as "bloody").

**Left** The refurbished, galleried interior of the Bleeding Horse

# THE PORTOBELLO

## 33 RICHMOND STREET SOUTH

The Portobello's history dates back to the building of the Grand Canal which would link Ireland's east and west coasts. Before the advent of roads and highways, the canal was the prime mover of goods through the country, with Portobello Harbour a major port for the barges. Work to build the canal began in 1756 and took almost forty years to complete. Where there was work, workers needed food and living accommodation and so along the canal new taverns began to appear. In 1793 the premises now known as the Portobello Hotel first opened.

The business had mixed fortunes, and several owners. William Lawlor took it over just prior to the Great Famine of the 1850s, when traffic on the canal reduced drastically. He was eventually forced to sell to avoid bankruptcy, and John Davy, who already owned premises in Baggot Street, saw in the arrival of the 20th century in the Portobello. Nationalism now began to sweep the country and rebels planned an armed insurrection to end British rule in Ireland. Davy, a magistrate, was at the time pro-British, especially as much of his business was generated by the nearby Rathmines army barracks.

One of Davy's barmen in 1916 was 25-year-old James Joyce of Grove Road – no relation to the writer – who joined the Irish Citizen Army, one of several nationalist paramilitary groups. Davy refused to give his barman the time off to attend training sessions, which took place on Sundays, but Joyce would often either pretend to be ill or simply fail to show up for work.

The Easter Rising of 1916 was initially planned for Easter Sunday, and Joyce again failed to turn up for work but the rebels leaders postponed it a day to Easter Monday, a bank holiday, when the city would be nearly deserted.

On the morning of Monday 24 April the rebels, including Joyce, gathered at the Irish Citizen Army's headquarters in Liberty Hall on the north quays of the River Liffey. At noon, the rebels (only 1500 of them instead of the planned 20,000) began to march off to seize targets around the city. Joyce and seven other rebels set off through the city, passing St Stephen's Green where another detachment under Countess Markiewicz seized the College of Surgeons. They continued up Harcourt Street and narrowly avoided capture at the junction of Adelaide

**Above** The Portobello – built on Dublin's Grand Canal in 1793

Road where a squad of mounted British soldiers met them.

Because of his knowledge of the area and the Portobello itself, Joyce's mission was to seize the pub and pin down soldiers trying to leave the Rathmines barracks. When he entered the pub, Joyce was confronted by his boss who said, "You've missed one too many Sundays. You can take it that you're on a week's notice." To which Joyce replied, "You can take it from me that you have seven seconds to get out. This premises is being seized in the name of the Irish Republic." Davy stood behind the counter, amazed at the young man's statement, but when Joyce levelled his rifle at him and then fired a shot at the mirrors behind the counter, Davy and his customers fled the premises.

The next few hours were taken up with securing the premises and setting up sniping positions in the windows facing down the Rathmines Road. Soon afterwards commanders realised what was happening across the city and when the first troops were sent out, the rebels in the Portobello pinned them down. The troops had to go into the city the long way around through Harold's Cross, giving the rebels time to dig in for the battle to come.

On Tuesday, the British soldiers crouched down behind the Canal walls, brought up a submachine-gun and barraged the building for a number of hours. On Tuesday night they stormed it but found it empty. Because of his intimate knowledge of the premises, Joyce had some of the men break through the cellar walls into the premises next door until they reached a nearby lane. When the building could no longer be held, the rebels made their escape back to the main body of the Citizen Army in St Stephen's Green.

After the surrender of the rebels the following Saturday, Joyce was arrested and transported to a military camp at Frongoch in Wales where he served six months. Davy, meanwhile, returned to his pub and after repairing the damage caused by the British army, went back to his business.

Nationalist leader Michael Collins also used the bar as a meeting-point for the Irish Republican Brotherhood, despite knowing that Davy was a magistrate and would have had him arrested had he known who he was. Collins believed that what was right under their noses the British would never see. On the off-chance that he was recognised, he always kept his gun cocked under the table but never had cause to use it.

The Davys eventually sold their premises. In the 1980s the pub was bought by its current owners, Finian McDonnell and Phil Monaghan, who extensively renovated and expanded it. In 1998 they added a 25-bedroom hotel to their property and and expanded the pub itself.

It's now an ideal bolthole for discerning revellers, with echoes of the past in the paraphernalia adorning cabinets, windows and shelves. It's a very large pub and also a very hospitable one, and those of a curious disposition will find much to amuse themselves in the nooks and booths scattered throughout.

**Above** The Portobello's drawers and shelves would once have stored groceries

## TEMPLE BAR

# THE PALACE

21 FLEET STREET

The literary tradition of Irish pubs probably dates from the 18th century, when many publishers had their bookshops and printing offices in buildings which were also taverns. This was the case with publishers George Faulkner and the Grierson family, for instance. Many pamphlets, newsheets and political manifestos were also issued from offices located in taverns. It was even a custom at one point to conduct book auctions in such locations, and many booksellers brought their stock from England to sell them to the highest bidders.

The Palace's rich literary tradition is also bound up with its journalistic one, thanks to its proximity to the *Irish Times*. Journalists have long dropped in here to slake their thirst between (or during!) shifts, thus preserving the strong Irish link between the drink and journalism. Indeed, it has often been said that if a cub journalist's copy doesn't have a Guinness mark on it somewhere, he or she may well be in the wrong job.

In the 1940s its ubiquitous habitué was Robert Smyllie, then editor of the *Irish Times*. Smyllie didn't so much enter the pub as make an entrance. Looking somewhat like a walrus-moustachioed Benny Hill, Smyllie traded badinage with his partners here when they should have been submitting copy across the road, but Ireland's pub lore has been the better for their indulgences. He held court from 5pm every day in what was referred to as the "intensive care unit" of the pub.

In his book *Remembering How We Stood*, John Ryan compares Smyllie to a "stranded bull walrus". He alleges that the reason Smyllie and his colleagues spent so much time in here was because they had the disposable income to do so, and that the *Irish Times* put money in their pockets at a time when money was "as rare as hen's teeth". Also,

**Above** A high, etched-glass partition separates the Palace's bar and lounge

because there was a world war on, food was scarce so there wasn't much more to spend money on. Smyllie only broke with tradition once, Ryan tells us, leaving the Palace to make a foray up to McDaid's. Once there, however, he saw Brendan Behan standing on a table crooning 'I

Was Lady Chatterley's Lover' out of tune, and beside him Gainor Crist (the model for JP Donleavy's *The Ginger Man*) being sick into somebody's pint. He decided to beat a hasty retreat back to the Palace and was never seen at McDaid's again.

Other Palace patrons have included FR Higgins, John Betjeman, Austin Clarke, Flann O'Brien and Patrick Kavanagh. Brinsley McNamara, whose life was never the same after his inflammatory roman-a-clef, *The Valley of the Squinting Windows*, blew the lid off small town life, also drank here.

It was at the Palace that O'Brien received the inspiration for many of his *Irish Times* columns (written under the pseudonym Myles na Gopaleen), often acting

**Above** The Palace's back lounge is full of literary portraits, some of them ex-patrons

out the nucleus of his scripts after one too many. Occasionally he would drive home under the influence, and was once caught for drunk driving. On another occasion, in full view of a garda, he staggered towards a car he had parked outside the pub, fell into it and started to turn the ignition. He was arrested for being drunk in charge of a vehicle, but when the case came to court it transpired that there had been no engine in the car. The funny little man had exacted a revenge of sorts on the law.

The pub is characterised by wooden niches, a tiled floor, leaded glass and lots of partitions. The front bar is rather narrow but the back lounge, betraying overtones of a parlour, is cosy. The portraits of Ireland's literary and republican greats act as a nostalgic backdrop to the leisurely conversations that take place here. It's a little hideaway that's intensely itself, despite being situated in such a central location.

The Palace is still a melting-pot for those who like the liberal, open ended exchange of ideas, and if today's patrons aren't quite as dissipated as Smyllie, or the discussions quite as heated as the ones that took place during the literary renaissance of the 1930s and 1940s, a visit is still highly recommended.

# THE OLIVER ST JOHN GOGARTY

## 19-21 ANGLESEA STREET

Gogarty was a surgeon, a cycling champion, wit, playwright, and memoirist, but he's chiefly remembered today as the "stately, plump Buck Mulligan" of *Ulysses*. He wouldn't be entirely pleased with such a historical perspective, it must be said. He was also politically active during Ireland's war of independence, and offered a "safe house" to Michael Collins in Ely Place; the key was discovered on Collins's body after he was assassinated in 1922. Gogarty himself was kidnapped the following year. His captors were just about to shoot him when he jumped into the freezing Liffey and swam to safety on the other side. He was so thankful to the river for saving his life (it was too cold for his abductors to follow him) that he famously donated a pair of swans to it.

Dublin's self-styled "Left Bank" pub – there's a pun there, which will become clear in a moment – is popular with the trendy, with music provided on a daily basis and a general air of vivacity and chit-chat, but it also has much to offer those of a historical bent.

There's a stone-tiled floor, lots of attractive wood panelling and old signs hanging from the ceiling. The main bar's U-shaped counter is a remnant from the Green Room in the late-lamented Theatre Royal.

Artefacts such as wagon wheels, old beer barrels and tankards abound.

Stone steps lead up to the back bar, passing a little vestibule with lovely circular plaques of an old farthing and ha'penny, and sketches of playwright Sean O'Casey and Lady Lavery, the lady who used to adorn the old Irish currency. There are also glass cases here with various curiosities inside.

A few steps down now lead to the pub's second bar, which is a converted bank — as you are repeatedly made aware of by objects such as night

safes, and doors bearing inscriptions like Bullion Vault, Manager's Office, Platinum Vault and Foreign Exchange. You will also see an old-fashioned jukebox here, and an antiquated weighing scales and cash register.

Not everything here can be trusted: a portrait of the Right Honourable Andrew Jameson of whiskey distillers Jameson & Sons would have him being born in 1896 and dying in 1898 — which suggests he become a successful whiskey magnate before he died at the age of two. Some feat indeed.

**Above** The eclectic look at the Oliver St John Gogarty

# THE AULD DUBLINER

24-25 TEMPLE BAR

Drinkers often spill out into the street from this "mecca for bacchanalian fun", as proprietor TP Smith's promotional brochure puts it. He's also aware of the invaluable location he has, enjoying a prime corner presence in the heart of Temple Bar.

Temple Bar, a maze of narrow cobbled streets running from the Central Bank to the Liffey, was the site of a 10th-century Viking settlement. Later the land became the property of Augustinian monks. In the 18th century it was over-run with brothels and pubs, but turned into a throbbing business centre. It was in decline in the first half of the 20th century but today it positively throbs with life.

Named after Sir William Temple, the provost of Trinity College in the 17th century, it's one of the oldest areas of Dublin – and until recently, one of the most neglected. The plan in the 1960s was to raze it to the ground and turn it into a bus depot. CIE, the stage transport company, bought most of the area's buildings for that purpose, renting them out in the interim. As time went on, however, and the area started to develop a bohemian character, a movement to preserve it gathered momentum. Foremost among those who worked for Temple Bar's preservation is the former *Taoiseach* Charles Haughey, who was instrumental in creating the frisson we witness today. He imagined it would fare better as a cultural centre, and that's indeed what it is.

With its public squares and its swanky apartments, its art galleries, cyber cafés and quirky old curiosity shops, Temple Bar is now a hive of activity. In fact the area seems to have been a huge factor in Dublin's renaissance as one of the style capitals of Europe. Some wits refer to it as "Ibiza in the rain".

**Left** The Auld Dubliner – at the centre of Temple Bar's "bacchanalian fun"

The Celtic Tiger roars nowhere more fiercely than here, in more than 50 restaurants and 30 pubs. In fact it has roared somewhat too loudly in the past, with stag nights and hen parties taking place with increasing regularity – and wildness – in the late 1990s. At this time the area looked in danger of becoming something of a dumping-ground for lager louts (the new Vikings?), most of whom came from Britain. Pressure from the public and publicans has resulted in a moratorium of such Rabelaisian goings-on, but Temple Bar is still a noisy place at night if you live in the area and are trying to snatch forty winks.

Temple Bar has also been called Dublin's Left Bank, and this is perhaps an image it cultivates with a tad too much self-consciousness. It's a spectacularly popular haunt of tourists, particularly at night-time when the shoppers have departed to make way for perhaps one too many boulevardiers, and it's difficult to imagine that the plethora of upmarket cafés and bistros were once the sites of grubby warehouses and dilapidated chapels. The area has been used as a backdrop in such movies as *Far & Away* and *The Commitments*. One of its bistros, the Bad Ass Café, is where Sinead O'Connor worked as a waitress before she came to fame as a singer.

The Auld Dubliner is more than happy to exploit the area's popularity, and why not? If you're looking for somewhere to drop anchor before, during or after a jaunt round these cobblestoned streets, this is as good a bet as any of the myriad of pubs queueing up to receive your custom. It's also renowned for its traditional music and pub grub.

It has undergone a few image changes in its time, causing cynics to dub it the "Auld Foreigner"; at present it has the original floor (part floorboards and part stone flags) and exposed brick walls. Outside there's a mural of a docker wearing a captain's hat, looking at a dog urinating. Perhaps that earthy image will prepare you for the irreverent

atmosphere inside.

It's a lively place with lots of activity and lots to look at. Timber dominates the interior, embellished by arches and benches which come from old church pews. A little raised area behind the main island bar is ideal for young lovers or private *tête-à-têtes*. The rust-coloured walls and dark lighting can make it seem more Mexican than Irish.

Elsewhere there are alcoves, and many miniature paintings set against equally dark backdrops. On the stairs down to the toilets there are some fascinating sepia prints, as well as an assortment of oddities on display such as fishnets, saddles, a birdcage and water pump. Celtic designs decorate the ceiling of the upstairs bar.

# THE CLARENCE HOTEL

6-8 WELLINGTON QUAY

The Clarence dates back to 1852 and has traditionally been regarded as the place where country people who were "up for the day", as the expression went, had a bite and a sup before embarking on a day's business, or shopping. In 1992 the hotel was bought by Bono and The Edge of U2 fame. (Bono used to drink here in the old days with his Virgin Prunes friend Gavin Friday. He says he always liked it because it was one of the few hotels that didn't take exception to Gavin's offbeat dress sense.) Having bought it, they weren't short of cash to refurbish it, but they insisted on preserving the building's character while adding on contemporary artifacts. The Octagon Bar, with its wood-panelled walls and elegant decor, has now become the place to drink for celebrities and celebrity-spotters. The Kitchen nightclub is downstairs.

The refurbishment, completed in 1996, transformed the hotel from a 2-star property to a 50-bedroom, 5-star hotel. American white oak and Italian limestone rubs shoulders with cutting-edge design. Rooms have wrought-iron bedside lamps, nickel-plated desk lamps and king-size beds. You can hire a cellular phone if you wish, and there's satellite television, a mini-bar, PC/fax facilities and even a private safe. The latter item leaves one in no doubt about the size of the wallet you will need if you choose to sojourn here. The Penthouse Suite, which has brilliant views of the city and even an outdoor hot tub, will knock you back a cool £1450 per night.

**Right** The Clarence, once a traditional hotel bar, is now a celebrity venue

# THE NORSEMAN

29 EAST ESSEX STREET

Descended from a medieval inn, the Norseman lays claim to being the second oldest surviving pub in Dublin after the Brazen Head. It has a licensing heritage stretching back 300 years, and possibly even longer. During the late 1600s the Wooden Man Tavern stood on the site, taking its name from a gigantic oaken figure which stood close to the junction of Eustace Street and Essex Street. By the 1700s it had been renamed the Royal Garter. The United Irishmen were founded a few doors away from it to agitate for parliamentary reform and religious rights.

In the 1830s it was run by one Peter Kavanagh as a grocers-cum-tavern. Its next proprietor, James Monks, was unfortunate enough to own it during Ireland's famine years, when business was hard. It has since changed hands and names frequently. The current owner John Morris bought it in 1985 and after this the Norseman's prosperity began in earnest.

In 1991, during works to the road surface outside the pub after the area had become pedestrianised, some workmen came upon a well which was reputed to date from the 1500s. It was identified as the probable property of the Augustinian Holy Trinity friary, founded in the 13th century in nearby Cecilia Street. It was subsequently called St Winifred's Well, in honour of the Welsh figure who enjoys equal reverence to Ireland's St Brigid. (Ireland had close trading connections with North Wales in the 11th century.)

The discovery caused huge interest in the area known as Wood Quay and the Norseman was of course a beneficiary of this.

The pub also has literary reverberations. It's mentioned under a

former name in the Wandering Rocks episode of *Ulysses*, and also in Joyce's short story "Counterparts" where Farrington goes for a drink "in the dark snug of O'Neill's shop". Such a snug is now long gone, but when it was there it was accessible from a side door to Eustace Street and generally used by those too concerned about being seen in a tavern to line up in the main bar. In those days, well-off middle-class drinkers were rare, but money seems to be no object to the customers who stroll through these doors today.

A former salt-of-the-earth establishment, it has latterly become infected with the hipper-than-thou brigade, and some older patrons have accused it of selling out. It still carries a large element of the past with it, however, and for this we should be grateful. The original floor and portions of the bar have been preserved. As has the ceiling, albeit in embellished fashion.

**Above** The Norseman is featured in both *Dubliners* and *Ulysses*

## THE NORTHSIDE

# THE HOLE IN THE WALL

BLACKHORSE AVENUE

This is reputed to be the longest pub in Europe. It's also one of the most beautiful. It was established in 1681, and a plaque at the entrance vaunts it as "one of the oldest public houses in Ireland, which for centuries has offered hospitality to all who cared to enter its doors." Today it's still a truly remarkable establishment, run with efficiency and friendliness by proprietors PJ and Margaret McCaffrey, and affords new revelations at every visit.

A coaching house before it became a straightforward inn, it has a timber and plaster exterior which runs for some 330 feet. At the entrance a parchment in a glass case informs that "the Old Tavern standeth on the road that led to the house of Hugh Tyrell, First Baron of Castleknock". It further relates that the pub got its name from the time when soldiers of the Blackhorse Regiment were stationed in the Phoenix Park, which runs alongside its walls. The soldiers would procure drink from the eponymous hole in the wall, which meant they weren't breaching military regulations by entering licensed premises while on duty.

Immediately to the right as you enter the door is a snug, marked Cul de Sac. This is a snug with a difference: it's made of stone. Inside are sketches of all Ireland's presidents, and old tin advertising signs. There's also – fittingly – a circular hole in the wall through which drinks can be ordered from the bar.

There are six interconnected bars in all. The roaring log fires, innumerable curios, stained-glass windows and carved furniture give you a whiff of the old tavern as it must have looked in the 17th century. In the Coachouse Bar are two other snugs, facing each other like old train compartments. Hideaways don't come more quaint than these, and they fit perfectly into the traditional motif.

In such an environment, you might find yourself somewhat thrown by the modern music that comes through the speakers in some of the bars, or the sight of businessmen on mobile phones arranging deals as they finish their meal. These are ubiquitous evils today, but they cannot dampen the impression you'll carry away with you.

The Mezzanine Bar upstairs contains a slightly more formal dining area, with a huge oil painting of Charles I at the top of the stairs and another array of presidential sketches. Many Irish presidents have taken hospitality here, as have foreign ambassadors, and other dignitaries such as Winston Churchill.

**Above and left** The atmospheric, well-preserved interiors at the Hole in the Wall

# HANLON'S

189 NORTH CIRCULAR ROAD

Ll roads, they say, lead to Tara. A fair few of them lead to Hanlon's pub as well, for five major routes converge at this imposing edifice.

In the early 1900s the cattle market used to be here as well, which meant a large percentage of the customers were farmers. They would do their deals on the street outside, haggling over prices before the fabricated reluctance gave way to a grudging acceptance, the done deal ushered in with a spit on the hand before purchaser and vendor adjourned inside for a more convivial confirmation. The area was then affectionately known as Cowtown, and still is by long-time residents.

During this period Margaret Barry was a local character who played her guitar outside the door of Hanlon's and occasionally drank inside with her donations from passers-by. She was something of a precedent, as women at the time generally didn't enter such dens of iniquity. Another regular street musician was a man called Stoney, who drove everybody crazy because he only knew one song, "It's A Long, Long Way To Tipperary". Many's the time people wished he would actually go there and give them some peace. He too played only as long as it took him to earn the price of a drink.

The other main patrons were the drovers who earned a few pence from the cattle-dealers for looking after their beasts as they drank. There was also a contingent of affluent buyers from England producing large billfolds and enjoying the local colour as they waited for the heads on their pints of Guinness to settle, or

**Right** Hanlon's was once the tavern of choice for farmers visiting the local cattle market

ordered takeaways of whiskey which they stuffed into the large pockets of their trenchcoats.

Many riotous nights took place here after cattle fairs, but then tranquillity would return to the area, the cowpats on the road the only reminder of the recent activity.

The pub was established in 1896, and is built in a similar Georgian style to the rest of North Circular Road, where it's located. James Kelly had run a thatched cottage pub here before John Hanlon arrived and built the current premises. The pub was originally known as the Market House, for obvious reasons. It had a privileged 6am opening time to accommodate the large number of agricultural dealers who descended on the market at dawn. Hanlon ran a grocery here and bonded his own whiskey. He also had stables at the back of the pub.

Since then it has changed hands often, the most controversial owner being one William McLoughlin, whose religious fervour was so intense he insisted all his barmen kneel every night and recite the rosary with him. Those who refused received a lash.

In 1989 it was bought by Jim and Tom McCormack. They built a new lounge, and again refurbished the place in 1996 to celebrate 100 years of trading. Today there are carvery lunches and evening meals plus live music at night from Wednesday to Sunday.

An attractive, rambling pub that positively buzzes with atmosphere, it winds hither and thither and will entrance casual visitors and dedicated drinkers alike. Admire the stone walls, the attractive library, the bottles stacked in cabinets about the place, the football photographs festooned throughout. And perhaps, as you take in the heady aroma of your whiskey or the food on offer, imagine how preferable this is to the old Cowtown odours that used to waft past Hanlon's doors.

# GILL'S

555 NORTH CIRCULAR ROAD

This plain, unadorned bar was established by James Gill in 1920 on land once owned by Buck Jones, a rich 19th-century landlord who became notorious as a self-styled "hanging judge" sentencing people to death for minor offences such as sheep-stealing. (Jones was also said to have moonlighted as a highwayman and his ghost on horseback is rumoured to haunt the area on certain nights.) James' son Noel took the place over in the 1950s.

The pub's main claim to fame rests on the fact that it was Brendan Behan's local before he moved to the suburb of Crumlin. It was also the haunt of Behan's uncle, Paddy English, a man who refused to take his cap off even in bed. Another patron in times past used to wear the colours of both teams when football matches took place in the nearby Croke Park, so that he could cadge drinks off both groups of supporters, displaying the requisite colour depending on the company present.

Gill has many stories to tell of such customers. He remembers Behan as a young man, a windswept lad with everything to live for, banging his fist on the table as he made a point about politics. If he'd had an

**Above** Gill's was Brendan Behan's local before he moved out to the suburbs article accepted in a newspaper it would be drinks on the house for all, but then there would be the times he would be volatile, when commotions would inevitably arise.

After Behan moved to Crumlin in 1936 the place was quieter, but he made a nostalgic pilgrimage back each year, and these grew more melancholic as the price of fame and alcoholism began to tell on him. In the early 1960s he came in to brag about the fact that he had received an invitation to John F Kennedy's US presidential inauguration. During the few years before Behan died it was one of his most prized possessions. In the pub an inscription to him goes: "Whatever is the truth, whether he was a writer first and a revolutionary second or vice versa – he was, in the immortal phrase of the Dublin of his childhood, the heart of the roll."

Gill's is still an unprepossessing pub which makes no attempt to sell itself. Its patrons are salt-of-the-earth types who know what they want, and here they get it. But one senses that pubs like this once rang with much more passion before Eamon de Valera's brave new world of decentralisation in the 1930s broke up traditional Dublin communities to relocate them in the suburbs with their one-up-one-down semis and pocket-handkerchief lawns. "I remember a woman bawling her eyes out just because she had to go to Donnycarney, for God's sake," Gill reminisces, "never mind Crumlin. But of course at that time even Donnycarney was the sticks."

Gill also remembers the time when cattle used to come down North Circular Road "on the hoof" for export. One day a bullock caught his reflection in the pub window and charged right through the glass window. The customers scattered to the four corners except for one man, much the worse for drink, who remained unperturbed. He calmly looked at the bullock standing beside him, and said, "What are you having, mate?" The bullock's reply hasn't been documented.

# KAVANAGH'S

1-2 PROSPECT SQUARE, GLASNEVIN

Better known to most Dubliners as the Gravedigger's, this pub is situated hard by the "dead centre of Dublin", Glasnevin Cemetery. (The official name is Prospect Cemetery, but it's rarely called that.) The pub was opened in 1833 and has remained with the same family since then, a tally of six generations in all. It's a pleasant spot to rest ones weary limbs and contemplate, if not mortality, at least the notion that not all things change with time. Like, for instance, a pint of Guinness in this fine establishment.

The area has much of interest: not far away is Croke Park, Ireland's national football stadium, and the Botanic Gardens are just down the road. In the cemetery itself are the graves of many luminaries, including politicians Arthur Griffith, Michael Collins and Eamon de Valera.

In the early 1900s there were 4000 burials a year in this cemetery. It's here that the funeral of Paddy Dignam ends up in James Joyce's *Ulysses*, having started from his house in Sandymount on the Southside. The best-known of the many interesting features here is a 168ft tower erected in memory of Daniel O'Connell, who founded the cemetery; "the Liberator" as the great political emancipator was known, was buried here in 1847. Countess Markievicz, who became Britain's first woman MP when she was elected for Sinn Féin in 1918, is also buried here. Roger Casement's body was brought here in 1965, almost 50 years after he was executed in England for his attempts to end British rule in Ireland. A huge granite rock sits above the tomb of nationalist leader Charles Stewart Parnell, who was ruined after his affair with Kitty O'Shea created a scandal in 1889. Literary figures include Brendan

Behan, the Jesuit poet Gerard Manley Hopkins and Maud Gonne McBride, the woman who fascinated (and spurned) WB Yeats.

The pub is alleged to be haunted by a benign ghost, and there are many stories told of sightings of the said spirit – who sports a grey beard and a butterfly collar on his shirt – merrily sipping pints and bothering nobody.

John Kavanagh was the first proprietor. He had 25 children in all, three of whom went to fight in the American Civil War of the early 1860s. One of these, Joseph, came back and took over the running of the pub. Joseph's son John took over after him but showed more interest in drinking than managing. He died young and his widowed wife Josephine made a better fist of running the place. She left it to her son, also called John. By an unusual set of events, he was both uncle and stepfather to Eugene Kavanagh the present proprietor.

Eugene took it over in 1973. He remembers the time when it was a grocery shop, dispensing everything from tea and bread to snuff and spices. In those days the snug was mainly frequented by women dubbed "shawlies" after the black shawls they wore. Women who were embarrassed to be seen drinking in public – considering the stigmatisation that prevailed in such times – used to call at the bar with a can and the barman would fill it up with Guinness for them, and they would then carry it home.

Eugene left school at 13 to work in the Guinness brewery. When he took over the pub it was in a bad state. He's amused that film and TV people seek it out today because he remembers when it was, as he says, "a dirty kip" that people wouldn't look at twice. He remembers hens in the garden and an open range in the kitchen. He also remembers funerals with horse-drawn carriages and mourning coaches – and a time when robbing corpses and selling them to science for money was a fairly prevalent practice. (Watchdogs used to roam the cemetery and

lookout towers were built in efforts to catch bodysnatchers).
Kavanagh's was one of the last pubs to use corked bottles of stout,
which they had to steam-wash as well as label themselves.

In the old days the cemetery railings were very near one wall of the
pub. The gravediggers, thirsty from their arduous labours, used to put

**Above** With little light getting in, Kavanagh's has a hermetic atmosphere

their arms through the railings and knock on the wall for a drink. Sometimes they tapped at it with their shovels, or threw stones at it for the same purpose. The walls still carry the marks of some of these knocks. As time went by, a sort of code was established for the barman: a heavy tap, perhaps, for a pint, a light one for a whiskey. The drink was then brought out to the men. If they had been tipped generously from a funeral party, they could pay the barman in cash. If not, it went on the "slate", and was paid off on a weekly or monthly basis, depending on the drinker's circumstances, or pay-day. The gravediggers would probably have been sacked if such practices came to light, but a blind eye was generally turned.

Part of the pub has been modernised in a semi-compromise to those who like their creature comforts, but the main bar, which has featured in such films as *Quackser Fortune Has A Cousin in the Bronx* and Bob Hoskins' *The Woman Who Married Clark Gable*, is plain and unadorned. It also bears the original stone floor of its ancestry. It has swing-doors too, and wooden walls and benches. Little light seems to get in, which accentuates the hermetic atmosphere.

The drinkers comprise a faithful crew of regulars, which means "blow-ins" are eyed with some curiosity, if not disdain. The atmosphere is leisurely, the drinkers assuring you that the man who made time made lots of it. There are no gaming machines here, nor jukeboxes. For diversion, patrons throw rubber rings at a board with hooks on it. Evidence of its origins as a grocery shop is visible throughout, with spice boxes from the past lined up along the walls. It's also replete with snugs, giving it a vaguely conspiratorial air.

Kavanagh's has seen as much laughter as tears in its history. As many customers have come here to celebrate as to mourn, on either occasion lowering copious pints. As the old saying goes, "the only difference between an Irish wedding and an Irish funeral is one less drunk."

# THE CAT AND CAGE

74 DRUMCONDRA ROAD UPPER

There's been an inn on these premises since 1689, the year before the Battle of the Boyne in which the Protestant army of William III defeated the forces of the Catholic James II. It was a coaching inn at that time and indeed shod steeds for that very battle (now remembered as the only time two kings have fought for the English throne on Irish soil). The present edifice dates from around 1750.

In 1798 the landlord of the time, one Jim Coughlan, was flogged by British soldiers on suspicion of harbouring those on the run from the law for both political and criminal reasons. As a result it also lost its inn status in the early 1800s, and since then has operated solely as a licensed premises.

The playwright Sean O'Casey was a regular here when he was secretary of the Labour Movement in 1914, and he mentions it in his memoir *Pictures in the Hallway*. Irish *Taoiseach* Bertie Ahern had his first pint here and still drops in occasionally to join the merrymaking of the sporting contingent whose throats are hoarse from roaring their team on, and in sore need of a few hot whiskeys. Croke Park is in the area and the pub fairly hops with excitement on the night before a major football or hurling final. St Patrick's Teacher Training College is across the road, and many trainee teachers drink here, preparing for the traumas of classroom life with a few fortifying pints of stout.

It's generally a busy place, and also manages to grab the passing trade of those en route to or from the airport, which is nearby. Among the bric-à-brac in the windows are old urns, pitchers, books, hats, sewing-machines, pipes and weighing scales. Prints of old Dublin are scattered throughout, as well as many photographs of sporting stars. The service is friendly and efficient.

Despite its rather suburban location, it has literary connections with both Patrick Kavanagh and Brendan Behan. Kavanagh drank here when he was lodging in Drumcondra Road in 1939. The story goes that Behan and an artist friend of his were here one day, the latter having been commissioned to do a painting of the pub by the owner. They drank the money but the artist hadn't started the painting. Behan suggested to the artist that he should submit a painting of a similar pub he had done some time ago and pass it off as the Cat. The fake painting was of course recognised, and the proprietor demanded his money back. (He had given the artist an advance of half the amount.) The artist refused this request; Behan started clamouring for the other half of the money immediately and to avert a row, the pair of them were given drink in lieu of the amount. Unsurprisingly, it was an offer Behan didn't refuse.

# THE BRIAN BORU

5 PROSPECT ROAD, GLASNEVIN

"Hedigan: Family Grocer" reads the sign over the door. Well it's a while since the Hedigans served groceries here, but it still carries the aura of the past about it. This is immediately apparent from the large painting of Brian Boru himself outside. Bearded, and looking mightily defiant as he heads into battle, the 11th-century king of Ireland carries a crucifix in his hand, which he exhibits to the throng of people surrounding him. In fact the Brian Boru, or Hedigan's as it's also known, is the only pub in Ireland to have a cross over its entrance.

There's been a public house on this site for more than 200 years. The present building dates from the 1850s, and the front remains virtually unaltered. The pub came into the Hedigan family on Friday, 15 July 1904, when Patrick Hedigan from Gallbally, County Limerick put in a bid for it at a public auction. (A record of this event has been preserved and is displayed in the bar beside the carvery.) Patrick built up a thriving business, much of it due to the large funeral trade that came its way because of its location en route to Glasnevin Cemetery. He was also noted for his special Power's White Label whiskey which he blended to his own recipe and served from the wood or bonded himself. The pub has remained in the family to this day and is at present managed by his grandsons Michael and Peter.

Of course its main historical connection is with the eponymous king of Ireland, who fought his most famous battle on 3 April 1014. This was the date of the Battle of Clontarf where he defeated Mael Morda, the king of Leinster, who had plotted with King Sitric, the

Viking ruler of Dublin, to overthrow him. The Vikings had been threatening a large offensive for some time and the outcome of the battle was crucial for the future of Ireland. It was also a symbolic victory of Christianity over heathenism, and proof that the Irish could unite when necessary.

Boru's victory ended Viking expansion in Ireland, many of the Danes hiding away in Howth until they could be rescued by their compatriots. Others intermarried with the Irish while Sitric himself converted to Christianity.

More than 15,000 Danes were killed in the fighting, and 4000 of Brian's troops. His son Murrough was also killed that day, as was his grandson Turlough, who was found drowned in the Tolka estuary with his hands still gripping the hair of a Dane he had followed into the water. Brian himself died on this day too, though not in battle. (Aged 72, he had chosen a spectator's role) After the fighting was over he retreated to his tent to pray. There were five soldiers guarding him, but four of them, imagining the danger was over, left him to pursue some retreating Danes who were nearby. That left only one guard. He was slain by the Danish Brodir — one of the most hated figures in Irish history. He crept into Brian's tent and slashed his throat from behind as he lay praying. Legend would have it that the heinous act took place on the very site where this bar sits today.

Nearby are the Botanic Gardens, founded in 1795 by the Royal Dublin Society and spread over 50 acres of an estate that was once the residence of the poet Thomas Tickerell. Delights include the curvilinear glasshouses — awesome pieces of architecture quite apart from the function they perform. They were designed and constructed between 1839 and 1852 by Richard Turner, who also created the palm house in London's Kew Gardens. Hours can happily be whiled away strolling round the gardens, which also contain a vegetable garden and an orchard. All in all there are over 20,000 species of plants and shrubs, and sheltered walks along by the Tolka river, its eddying waters fanned by the weeping willows that droop down above them.

The Brian Boru is an elegant, neat-as-a-new-pin establishment, with a large central counter which extends into both lounges. Each is tastefully decorated, with sketches and photographs of literary and historical personages dotting the walls. There are brass lamps and stained glass (with a large "H" engraved on it) on both windows and doors. There are wooden grocery shelves behind the counter, and wood panelling throughout. Little alcoves greet you at every turn, with here and there a bookcase laden with old tomes.

The pub is a former recipient of the National Pub Catering Award, an Egon Ronay Award and continues to pride itself on the quality of its food and drink. There is also a conservatory and a beer garden at the back.

**Above** Dating from the 1850s, the Brian Boru has been in the Hedigan family since 1904

# SMYTH'S

12 FAIRVIEW

Proprietor Vincent Smyth has fashioned an emporium that has something for everyone: businessmen, bohemians, regulars and the passing trade. This is a beautifully finessed pub that's choc-a-bloc with characterful touches. The jewel in Fairview's crown, it has oodles of warmth and visual splendour. The wooden partitions on the right as you enter are exquisite, as are the enamel advertisements adorning them. The walls are awash with vivid recreations of scenes from the past – barefoot children at the turn of the last century, a cinema ad from 1932 – and the ubiquitous dark wood panelling acts as a fitting background.

Its first leasehold was in 1880. At that time it was largely used as a rest stop by the merchant families of Dublin, who enjoyed riding out to Clontarf and Howth in their horse-drawn carriages for day-trips at the weekend.

Nestled snugly in the heart of downtown Fairview,

**Above** Smyth's was a 19th-century stop-off for carriages day-tripping to Howth

Smyth's overlooks the extensive park of the same name and is within striking distance of the famous Point Theatre. It's an entrancing mix of wood and stone, and does a flourishing food trade, specialising in American cuisine, which includes dishes like Cajun Blackened Steaks and Charcoal Grilled Chicken Fillets.

The only discordant note struck by the pub is the pictorial recreation of the darkest moment in Fairview's history: the night the Germans

dropped four sets of bombs in the area, one of them leaving a huge crater in the middle of the road. The devastation was terrible: 38 people were killed, 100 more injured and more than 800 lost their homes. Ireland was neutral in World War II and Germany later issued an apology, but it couldn't bring back the dead, or console the maimed. It remains a raw subject with people all over Dublin, and there are even said to be a handful of people still alive who were in this pub the night it happened.

# CLONTARF CASTLE

CASTLE AVENUE

Clontarf Castle is a hotel rather than a pub proper, but it's a fascinating place to have a drink. One of the most imposing structures in Dublin, it mixes the military, the ecclesiastical and the domestic, and commands the surrounding landscape like a colossus. A stone arch frames the entrance to the grounds, and a lamplit avenue leads to the castle itself, watched over by a huge black brass lion doing sentry duty outside.

A castle was first built here by Hugh de Lacy in 1172 after he was made Lord of Meath by Henry II. In 1307 it passed into the hands

of the Knights of St John of Jerusalem, an order of military monks who helped the poor on their journeys to the Holy Land. It changed hands many times over the next few centuries, with events such as Oliver Cromwell's plundering of the country in 1649.

The building was declared unsafe in 1835 and architect William Morrison was called in to survey it. He noticed that the foundations were sinking, so he ordered it to be knocked down. It was rebuilt afterwards, being completed two years later in roughly the neo-Gothic style in which we see it today.

**Above** The Knight's Bar at Clontarf Castle

It was home to various members of the Vernon family for some 300 years but after the male line failed in the early 1900s it passed into the hands of George Oulton. After his death it was left uninhabited for 10 years until 1960, when it was bought by the current owners Gerry and Carmel Houlihan. They started catering for wedding parties, and also hitched themselves onto the cabaret bandwagon, which was just beginning to become big at that time. The last cabaret show was staged in 1997; the place was given a massive overhaul and reopened in June 1998 as the medieval fantasy extravaganza it is today.

There are a staggering 111 rooms in all. A glass case at the entrance displays a copy of an 1840 edition of the *Irish Penny Journal*, which reads: "Such architectural works are not interesting merely for the gratification they afford to the feeling of taste, and the epic beauty and dignity which they contribute to landscape scenery, but have a higher interest as pledges to the nation than those who have erected them have a filial attachment to the soil which gave them birth." This is a profound expression of the deep effect this majestic building has on anyone who spends time here.

In the giant foyer, a large open fireplace stands opposite the main reception area, and beside it a piano and another brass lion. Surrounding you are huge wooden pillars, stags' heads, stuffed pheasants hanging from a window ledge and portraits of wigged historical figures on the walls. There's also a stone snug through which you can glimpse a bunch of logs on an ancient hearth.

The two main bars are the Knight's Bar and the Drawbridge Bar, the former more ornate and the latter more rustic. A television spoils the spell of antiquity somewhat, but it's not too intrusive. The hotel also has a gym and a business centre.

The area of Clontarf gets its name from the Gaelic *cluain tarbh*, "meadow of the bull". The bull reference comes from nearby Bull Island, so named because of the fierce strength of the waves pounding upon the shore.

**Left** The gigantic foyer continues the medieval theme at Clontarf Castle

# DOLLYMOUNT HOUSE

366 CLONTARF ROAD

This massive seafront establishment does a roaring trade, and if you drop in at lunchtime you'll be hard put to find a seat. It's easily distinguishable by its distinctive yellow and wine exterior and attractive lanterns, as well as numerous stained-glass designs with a maritime motif that befits its location by Bull Island.

It opened as a fisherman's tavern in 1782, and has had its ups and downs. In the 1800s one of its proprietors went bankrupt after he spent his money refurbishing the place, but when one Michael Monaghan bought it in the early 1900s it did prosperous business. During World War I it acquired a reputation for housing ladies of, let us say, dubious virtue; their main customers were the British soldiers who were stationed in the area. Leo Mulligan, the present proprietor, bought it in 1988 and promptly set about refurbishing it to its present splendour.

Everywhere you look you'll see something nautical: ships' steering-wheels, clocks, speedometers, a giant model of a ship in the centre of the bar, and a 6ft-long model of a currach, traditionally made of waterproofed hides over a wicker frame, framed by two portholes cut through the wall. There are other model ships in glass cases.

Every day, multitudes drive up to eat and drink their fill in a thoroughly commodious environment. Five minutes away from the pub is the aforementioned Bull Island, an area of dune grassland accessible by a boardwalk and the splendiferous Dollymount Strand, a huge expanse of beach which is also open to cars. (Many of Dublin's motorists have had their first driving lesson on this strand.) There's also a causeway that was built in 1819 by Captain William Bligh (he of the *Bounty* fame – or infamy) to stop Dublin Harbour from silting.

The water isn't clean enough to swim in but the spot nonetheless offers a brilliant view of Howth. If the day is windy enough you may spot enterprising windsurfers braving the choppy waves, or people struggling with sophisticated kites on the strand. Fitness enthusiasts make good use of it, and those training for athletic or sporting events.

A long boardwalk leads to the pier, at the end of which stands Poolbeg Lighthouse. From here ferries can be seen coming and going from nearby Dublin Port to Holyhead on Anglesey, in Wales. You will usually see fishermen here as well, trying their luck from the boardwalk and the beach.

Bull Island is also a haunt for birdwatchers. There's a nature reserve with up to 30,000 shore birds at times, wildfowl and wading birds proliferating in the mudflats and saltmarshes. Kestrels and peregrines can also be seen here, as can sparrowhawks and owls. Others are more interested in the two golf clubs: St Anne's and Royal Dublin.

**Above** Originally a fisherman's tavern, Dollymount House maintains a nautical feel

# THE SOUTHSIDE

# THE PATRIOTS INN

760 SOUTH CIRCULAR ROAD, KILMAINHAM

A 10ft-wide sign outside the door of this lively establishment boldly states: "This old pub standeth on sacred ground, surrounded by the high walls of the Royal Kilmainham Hospital, by the ancient cemetery of Bully's Acre and the dungeons of Kilmainham Jail. The Patriots Inn has been closer to the pulse of Irish history than any contemporary pub." Few would question this claim.

There's been an inn on the site since 1793, when the enterprising John Ward felt business would accrue to it from the jail (which had opened the year before) and also from the cemetery, grieving and drinking being two activities the Irish seem fond of engaging in simultaneously. Bully's Acre cemetery was situated in the grounds of the Royal Hospital, a home for retired and/or disabled soldiers. The timing of the building of the jail was significant because the French Revolution had recently taken place and the British felt (rightly as it turned out) that the ideals it espoused might also take root in Ireland. Six years later the 1798 rebellion occurred, and when the rebels were captured it was here they were incarcerated.

Ward's son, also called John, took the pub over, renaming it the Victoria Tavern in honour of Queen Victoria after she acceded to the British throne in 1837. The main customers at this time were the veterans from the hospital. Soon the Great Southern and Western Railway was built and its workers boosted its trade further.

**Right** The Patriots was built in 1793 to take custom from those visiting Kilmainham Jail

In 1856 Margaret Drummond bought the pub, taking advantage of the original inn licence to lodge travellers and relatives of those residing in what she called "the Big House" (the jail) across the way. Because of the unique circumstances, she was also allowed to open the premises at 5am. The Murray family took the pub over in 1898, changing its name once again, this time to the Kilmainham Tavern. Guinness was now served here for the first time.

After the Easter Rising of 1916, most of the captured insurrectionists were interred in Kilmainham. Indeed, it was said that their screams could be heard in the pub as they were being executed. One of the most poignant executions was that of the poet Joseph Mary Plunkett. He was married by candlelight just two hours before he was shot, the ceremony taking place as soldiers stood to attention beside bride and groom, their rifles cocked. Éamon de Valera, who went on to become Ireland's prime minister and later its president, was also held here at this time. He was originally sentenced to death for his part in the Rising, but the sentence was subsequently commuted because of his mixed heritage. (He had Spanish blood, and was born in America).

The Civil War of 1922 was also traumatic for the pub, which was riven – as the country was – by divided loyalties. The numbers in the jail again swelled in the aftermath, but two years afterwards it was closed for good, to the jubilation of all. De Valera was its last prisoner.

The pub has had many more owners since then, and also further name changes; it was called the Patriots in 1989, and is currently owned by the trio of Vincent Stapleton, Joe Doyle and Patrick Kavanagh – no relation to the poet. It owes much of its fame to its location, of course, but it's also a pleasant place to have a pint.

It was renovated with Liscannor marble some years ago. The bar is L-shaped, snaking its way around corners. The walls, as one might have expected, are literally dotted with pictures and sketches of

Kilmainham Jail: entrance, exercise yard, courtyard and so on. One sketch, entitled simply "The Condemned Cell", sends a shiver down the spine. All it shows is a hearth, a table and a stool, but it's eerie in its spartan suggestiveness.

The snug, dubbed "The Cell" because of its barred top, is rather cluttered with a profusion of stools, but these, coupled with a round table in the middle, make it suitable for many more people than the average snug, which rarely caters for more than a half dozen people. Its walls are a veritable shrine to Ireland's favourite patriot Michael Collins, with framed photographs of him in military and casual garb and a host of tributes from various writers attesting to his guile, charm and leadership qualities.

Here also there's a framed edition of the *Irish Times* (then called the *Weekly Irish Times*) of 29 April 1916, with the headline "Sinn Fein Rebellion in Ireland" and the subtitle "The Darkest Week in the History of Dublin". Another framed page features the details of the Rising: the fighting in the GPO, an early attempt to blow up Nelson's Pillar, the attack on Dublin Castle and the "gunboat action" in Ringsend.

There are also many photographs of the old Royal Hospital. One, taken in about 1900, features a row of the disabled soldiers, sitting in line like so many ancient mariners. Today the "RH" is a cultural centre which specialises in exhibitions, lectures and concerts. It's Ireland's only surviving fully classical 17th-century building. The building was extensively renovated in the 1980s but has preserved its magnificent classical structure fronting onto a central courtyard. An elegant clock tower is set in the front quadrangle.

The jail has undergone a similar change of function. It remained closed until 1966, the 50th anniversary of the Rising, when it was opened as a shrine to the martyrs. Today there are guided tours and audio-visual shows documenting seminal events of Ireland's history.

# THE PENNY BLACK

TYMON NORTH, TALLAGHT

Purpose-built pubs don't always work; this one does. Genial proprietor Hugh Brady presides over this handsome establishment located in the foothills of the Dublin Mountains in the ever-expanding suburb of Tallaght. He and his co-manager John

**Above** The Penny Black in the foothills of the Dublin Mountains

Purcell bought the site in 1987 and set about designing the pub in mock-historic format. This they have achieved with more than a modicum of style.

The clock tower makes it look like a church (it was mistaken for one during its construction), but there the ecclesiastical theme ends. Inside a postal one takes over, the name of the pub referring to Britain's first uniform rate of postage in 1837. Hugh has an 1840 edition of a Penny Black stamp framed behind the bar; the fact that it has been cancelled (by the Maltese Red Cross) increases its value in his eyes, and also the fact that it isn't serrated.

The postal motif is evident elsewhere, with an original postbox in the foyer, sketches of postmen in traditional garb from the 16th century onwards, and a pictorial history of stamps through the ages in an area designated the Postman's Snug. Another snug features old prints of Nelson's Pillar before it was blown up by the IRA in 1966 on the 50th anniversary of the Easter Rising and trams trundling down O'Connell Street (then known as Sackville Street).

The two snugs are oases in a large bar that's very simple in its structure but also very pleasing. An air of camaraderie is evident, and the standard of both food and drink is exemplary. The seating areas are neatly sectioned off, a testament to the good planning which doesn't detract from the "big happy family" effect the pub exemplifies.

# THE MORGUE

TEMPLEOGUE VILLAGE

A treasure-trove of Victoriana, this was first licensed in 1848, a time that was one of the grimmest chapters in Ireland's history. For some five years after 1845 the potato crop upon which the poor desperately depended for sustenance failed recurrently, thereby plunging the country into a nightmare of death and disease. One might imagine the pub's name to have resulted from this circumstance, but in fact the Templeogue Inn, as it was then called, provided support to famine victims during their time of trial.

The pub garnered a different type of recognition 40 years later when the Dublin-Blessington Steam Railway made its first stop here on its inaugural journey in 1888, thereafter using it as a ticket office. A tram depot was built here as well, and this provided tickets and refreshment facilities for passengers until 1932. During its lifespan, however, the 12-mile tramway acquired the unfortunate nickname "the Longest Graveyard in the World", because of the many casualties on the line. Numerous inquests were held into accidents, resulting in the pub performing a subsidiary function as a kind of makeshift morgue. Many of the accidents took place as a result of overcrowding, a situation which caused one doggerel poet to emote:

*The battle of Ypres was only a sham*
*Compared to the rush for the Blessington Tram.*

In the pub are many pictorial records of the tramway, as well as a stained-glass message warning us to beware of it. As if to emphasise the theme, tattered old suitcases hang from the walls, and there are also old train timetables and a carriage-like area with leather seating. Other themed pictures feature pub fronts and bridge motifs, and there's a lounge with paintings of nothing other than drinkers, which ought to put you in the mood to tarry here a while.

There are snugs aplenty for intimate chats, and all forms of bric-à-brac on shelves and in glass cases. The pub is a haven for sporting enthusiasts, as is evidenced by the set of golf clubs that are nailed to the wall beside the counter, and the rugby pictures in the hallway. The Templeogue Tennis Club is next door, and after a knockabout many players enjoy a cool drink in the beer garden at the back. Additional attractions include food from 3pm onwards Monday to Saturday and a Sunday carvery that stays open until 6.30pm.

**Above and next page** The Morgue once doubled as the local railway ticket office

# THE GLENSIDE

LANDSCAPE ROAD, CHURCHTOWN

Until the 1980s the pub on this site was just another routine one doing a modest trade. When brothers Paul and Tom Mangan bought it in 1983, however, they had some dramatic ideas for boosting business. They revamped it extensively under the auspices of architect Frank Ennis, breaking down the existing structure into sectioned-off booths and scouring the country for rustic artefacts with which to decorate it. More importantly still, they decided to put a thatched roof on it. The final bill came to close on £1 million, but it was a sound investment. The pub went on to win many awards. It's open to the charge of overkill, but one can't deny there is much of interest here.

**Above** The Glenside – an unashamedly themed Irish country pub

185

The area was once called Badger's Glen, and the pub's name loosely stems from this. The tone is set from the outset by a mural on the outside wall of one of John Gilroy's classic Guinness ads: a man with a tray of stout, being pursued by a lion who seems to fancy the drink almost as much as he does. Above is the thatched roof which has given the pub its fame, being the largest in Ireland.

Inside, items such as butter churners and bellows pop up willy-nilly on the walls, as do multifarious street signs, weighing scales, rifles, radios, taps, bodhrans and even a lumberjack's chainsaw. Glass cabinets display models of vintage cars; in one corner, there's a library of sorts, spilling over with old books, some of which have been disappointingly

**Above and right** Old bottles and signs fill every available inch of space

cut to fit the rather narrow shelves. In a lamplit snug with a sloping ceiling are sepia pictures of Dublin's past.

In the front bar, little cubicles behind the counter hark back to the days when pubs tended to double as groceries. There are Celtic designs on the stained glass here, and enamel ads for products like Sweet Afton and Fry's choice confectionery. More pictorial representations of long-gone products line the stairs to the upstairs bar, along with a collection of film posters.

The upstairs lounge perhaps overgilds the lily. Constructed something like a huge hay barn, it's bedecked with a plethora of curios: wagon wheels, coaching lamps and farm implements, messenger boys' bicycles, a blacksmith's forge, a cobbler's last, an old gas meter, a harness and a saddle, a spinning machine. "Cross The Railway By Footbridge" reads a large sign. Even the jukebox is a vintage model (though the music emanating from it is contemporary).

Some people find the place magical while others see it as contrived. The answer is perhaps somewhere in between. A lot of effort, whether misplaced or not, has gone into the reconstruction of this pub by the Mangans, who also own the Stone Boat and Doheny & Nesbitt's. They enjoy a flourishing trade and place a large emphasis on the culinary aspect of the pub, catering for the business class by day and the more casual diner in the evenings.

## NORTH OF DUBLIN

# THE ABBEY TAVERN

HOWTH

The picturesque headland fishing village of Howth has reputedly been inhabited since 3250BC. Its name comes from *hoved*, the Norse word for "head". Norman nobleman Almeric Tristram acquired the ancient Howth Castle in 1177 and it has remained in the same family ever since, though the male line ended in

**Above** The Abbey Tavern looks on to the picturesque harbour front at Howth

1909. Howth Harbour dates from 1807 and until 1833 was the main crossing point to Holyhead in Wales (when the bay silted up, Dun Laoghaire took over this service).

It was here that George IV docked on a visit to Ireland the year of his coronation in 1821. Howth is also where, in 1914, Erskine Childers brought 900 rifles in his yacht the *Asgard* to help the republican cause. (During the Civil War of 1922, Childers was court-martialled and executed by his former nationalist colleagues.)

On weekdays out of season Howth looks for all the world like a sleepy, sparsely populated village, but it comes to life at night. It has a marina with a local fishing fleet, and a transport museum with old

**Above** A section of the Abbey Tavern was originally part of a 15th-century seminary

trams, fire engines and double-decker buses.

Another attraction is the grounds of the aforementioned Howth Castle, where there's a large *cromlech*, or prehistoric burial site. The

castle itself is not open to the public, but you can visit the gardens, which contain more than 2000 rhododendrons spread out over a 30-acre site. According to the legend, Grace O'Malley, the Queen of Connacht, visited the castle in 1575 on her way back from visiting Elizabeth I in England. She was anxious to have something to eat but was informed that people were too busy to cater for her. As revenge (this was a lady who didn't like to be rebuffed), she kidnapped the son of the house, returning him only when Lord Howth, the proprietor of the time, promised her he would never again refuse visitors. As a result of this, Howth publicans and hoteliers strive to prevent history repeating itself.

Those of a more athletic bent might prefer to trek around Howth Head. Leopold Bloom proposed to Molly from these vertiginous slopes in James Joyce's *Ulysses*. She felt his heart beating against her as she uttered her famous affirmation at that book's conclusion, and you may feel the same excitement as you

**Above** The Abbey Tavern bar

view the huge expanse of sea around you. Many think it one of the most beautiful views in the world. From the cliff path, on a clear day, you can even see the Wicklow Mountains in the distance.

The small island of Ireland's Eye is also nearby, and boats take visitors across to it. It's uninhabited, but has an old stone church dating from the 6th century, and a Martello tower designed to provide coastal defence. The island is now a bird sanctuary.

The Abbey Tavern is situated just 50 yards from Howth harbour, halfway up the hill. Part of the building dates back to the 15th century when it was built as a seminary for the local monks. The atmosphere now is cosy, perhaps too cosy, and the set-up could be accused of being formulaic, but despite (or maybe because of) this the pub acts like a magnet for visitors anxious to grab a flavour of Ireland's past in a suitably nautical setting.

This is the quintessential "olde worlde" pub: stone walls, open fireplaces, flagstone floors and furnished with old church pews. It was bought by James Scott-Lennon in 1945 and is now run by that man's grandson and namesake.

Since the 1960s the Abbey Tavern has specialised in musical evenings geared particularly towards visitors from abroad. This has resulted in its worldwide renown. You'll frequently see busloads of foreigners with sunglasses and camcorders disappearing through its doors, looking forward to a five-course dinner followed by traditional music. Seafood is, of course, a speciality. In 1956, the owners of the Abbey opened the Abbot Restaurant next door and this is now thriving as well, in a similarly traditional atmosphere.

After you've partaken of your fill you may care to walk the nearby pier and watch the waves crashing against the rocks. You could also visit Howth Abbey, originally a church founded by Sitric, the Norse King of Dublin in 1042.

# DUFFY'S

MAIN STREET, MALAHIDE

Malahide is one of the most scenic parts of north Dublin, and boasts a beautiful marina. It is also one of Dublin's most expensive areas, with some of the properties running into the million-pound bracket.

**Above** Duffy's has won several awards for its frontage

From the 5th to the 9th century, Malahide's peace was shattered by small armies of Vikings who regularly raided the harbours and also used the village as a base from which to attack Dublin. The most interesting attraction is Malahide Castle, which dates back to the 12th century and sits in 250 acres of parkland (also open to the public). Its gardens contain more than 5000 species of flowers stretching over 20 acres.

The castle has been occupied by the Norman-Irish Talbot family since 1174 when Richard Talbot captured the surrounding land. There are turrets, Gothic windows, beautiful wood panelling and variegated artefacts. The Great Hall has a huge painting of the Battle of the Boyne of 1690, in which James II sought to regain the English crown from the Protestant William and Mary. The Talbots were on the losing side in this, being Catholics. It's said that 14 members of the family sat down to breakfast here on the morning of the battle and not one returned. As in all the best castles, there's even a family ghost who appears from time to time – this one's name is Puck.

Duffy's, situated in the heart of Malahide, once traded as a provisions store, and bottled and distilled its own whiskeys and beers. It also doubled occasionally as a makeshift morgue, mainly for maritime casualties. Malahide has traditionally been famous as a coal importing port, and since this was thirsty work and done early in the morning, the pub was allowed to open at 7am to service the workers when they had completed their labours.

In the 1950s the pub was owned by one James Hogan, and when he died in 1962, in a fit of generosity he left it to his staff. Six years later it passed into the hands of the Duffy family, where it has remained. Famous for its huge wall mural of the beach at Malahide, it's has now become one of the "in" places for the trendy set.

# THE LORD MAYOR'S

MAIN STREET, SWORDS

From the outside, this thatched-roofed emporium looks as if it goes underground, as the landscape slopes dramatically from its front door to the car park at the back. Inside, however, it's a model of symmetry, the seating area being attractively set off with a slew of hatches and pillars, the latter carrying ads for products long gone off the market: Golden Shred marmalade, Hafner's sausages, Clunes Sarsfield Plug, Kilkenny beer and Senior Service cigarettes.

There's a glass case featuring a selection of currency from around the world. Elsewhere there are photographs of historical scenes: a football match at Croke Park in 1955, the Swords Emergency Fire Services, some World War II pictures and the Harford steam engine en route to Kilmainham and Poolaphouca in 1945.

The open fireplace has a wooden mantel and is surrounded by books and bric-à-brac, the walls here having a rough brown-wash effect which is very toney. More interesting still is the bar counter which has been composed of railway sleepers. On top is a range of wooden barrels and some intricate wood panelling.

Originally known as the Royal Oak, it dates back to 1668, which makes it the oldest tavern in Swords by far. There used to be a turnpike gate nearby, which meant it grabbed all the custom from commuters on the Dublin to Drogheda highway, especially those anxious to rest their heads in mid-journey. At this time it also had a courtyard where farriers wiped the sweat off the steeds. Inside, meanwhile, their owners let off a different kind of steam – with a tad more jollification.

**Left** The bar at Duffy's, Malahide

# THE BOOT INN

PICKARDSTOWN, CLOGHRAN

You would be hard put to better this for authenticity. With its thatched roof and lanterns outside the door, you immediately feel yourself transported back into history. The fact that the frontage looks somewhat run down even adds to that sense. "Ye Olde Boot Inn" says the sign, which used to have an actual stone boot beside it. The door is divided in the middle, in the old barn-door style.

An atmospheric, low-ceilinged alehouse located at the back of Dublin Airport, it dates back to 1593. Inside is displayed the text of an old parchment citing a reference to the pub by one William Brereton, a Cheshire baronet who stayed here in the 17th century. "Here wee lodged," he wrote, "at ye sign of ye boote, a taverne, and was well used, and found it far better accommodation in so meane a village than could be expected."

James II and King William are reputed to have drunk here. Daniel O'Connell, who led the movement for Catholic Emancipation in the early 1800s, used to stay here on his way to speaking engagements in the North. The pub was on the main highway to Belfast, which explains its popularity with so many VIPs of the era.

As befits what was once an old country tavern, there's an open fireplace with old kettles and pots adorning it, but the equine theme is uppermost here. On the walls are pictures of horses and hunters, harnesses, a hunting horn, a bugle, and a brass spit which hunters used for roasting their kill of the day. In the cellar are stuffed foxes and hares in glass cases, as well as an array of old implements which taverns like this used for bottling their own ale.

An interesting photograph shows nationalist leaders Michael

**Right** The Boot Inn, dating back to 1593, is reputed to have played host to kings

Collins, Eamon de Valera and Arthur Griffith at a hurling match in Croke Park in 1914, all looking very merry. What makes the picture intriguing is the fact that all three were on the run from the British forces at the time, and here they were enjoying a day out in full view of everyone. Elsewhere is a portrait of Robert Emmet, who was executed in 1803 for his nationalist activities. The painting is footnoted with the following poetic tribute to him from Thomas Moore:

*He had lived for his love,*
*for his country he died*
*They were all that to life*
*had entwined him.*
*Nor soon will the tears of*
*his country be dried*
*Nor long will his love stay*
*behind him.*

Upstairs is a function room which commands panoramic views of the airport. There's also a discotheque attached, where an entirely

**Above and right** The Boot Inn was once a popular stop on the main highway to Belfast different kind of hunting goes on.

Make sure you have a good map for this one as it's well off the beaten track. From the city centre head for the Dublin Airport main roundabout. Go straight across it and continue until you see the Coachman's Inn on your right. Go left at the next roundabout and stay on this road for a mile and a half until you reach the next roundabout. Turn left here and then take the next left again, where you'll find the Boot Inn on the left-hand side of the road.

# THE COACHMAN'S INN

AIRPORT ROAD, CLOGHRAN

This very large, rambling and busy pub is within spitting distance of Dublin Airport. Located in Cloghran (Gaelic for "stony place") just off the main Dublin-Belfast motorway, it does a flourishing trade with commuters, the business class, and anyone who enjoys a pint in a harmonious environment.

When it was established in the 1790s, its main function — apart from servicing its clients — was quartering horses in mid-journey. In the 1880s it was sold to the Haughey family (no relation to Ireland's former *Taoiseach*), who succeeded in procuring a 4am opening time to suit local market gardeners travelling in to the city. It also had permission to stay open all night on Wednesdays, because this was the night before cattle dealers decamped for the Stoneybatter mart.

The Radcliffe family took over in the early 1900s and replaced the thatched roof with a galvanised one. They also ran a forge next door, specialising in shoeing horses. It has had several owners, and several different names, since then, but by the 1960s it was known as the Coachman's Inn. Its present owner, Hugh Curran, has been instrumental in an extensive revamping of its interior.

There are two levels, each large, and a horseshoe-shaped bar over which sits a statuette of a black lead coach. On the shelves are curios such as old plates, copper pots, weighing scales, pitchers and urns. The beamed roof is pyramid-shaped, with friezes on the pinnacle. There's even a frieze effect on the wooden floor, though this is somewhat faded now. The stone walls carry pictures of hunters riding to the hounds, or preparing to, and also a set of aviation pictures as befits its proximity to the airport. There's an old-fashioned stove as well, and various cabinets containing other interesting artefacts. Upstairs is a smaller bar kitted out with pictures of animals. Wood is predominant here, and there are two cute windows positioned so low they're practically on the ground. Next door is a smart restaurant.

**Above and next page** The Coachman's Inn once quartered travellers and their horses

# THE HUNTSMAN INN

GORMANSTOWN

Irish comedian Colin Murphy has a gag that goes, "The mammy told me to go down to the pub to get an old typewriter. I asked her where my bike was and she said, 'Nailed to the ceiling like it always is!'"

The point is well made. All too often pubs today – in desperate search of a connection with the past – over-egg the omelette, with tragicomic results. The Huntsman, a 300-year-old, stone-flagged establishment, could be accused of such opportunistic fussiness, but it isn't flash or crass.

The eponymous huntsman is captured in a wall mural outside with a beer in his hand; inside, every few feet there are stuffed animals of some sort – rabbits, stoats, owls and so on – as well as endless

**Above** The Huntsman – a 300-year-old thatched tavern

numbers of old watches, clocks, dolls, toys and artefacts in the glass cubicles surrounding all the partitions. High up on the shelves you'll see pitchers, urns, bottles, old wirelesses, a ship in a bottle, you name it. There are also any number of old advertisements for products you might never have heard of. Hung from the ceiling are cartwheel chandeliers and a 3ft-wide airplane. There's even a traditional phone booth which looks as if it's been plucked off an old street and plonked down here. Some tables are made from the bases of antique sewing-machines; one is actually an old beer barrel. You don't get the impression of these being tacked on to the premises; they're part of it.

**Above and right** The Huntsman has an eclectic taste for bric-à-brac

## SOUTH OF DUBLIN

# THE PURTY KITCHEN

OLD DUN LAOGHAIRE ROAD, DUN LAOGHAIRE

D ating back to 1728, this is one of the oldest pubs in Dublin after the Brazen Head and the Norseman. It was originally called the Dunleary Inn, and served as a lodging-house for those about to depart for England from the nearby port. In subsequent years it was a grocery and coffee house.

The structure now is disarmingly simple, a horseshoe-shaped bar looking out on a perfectly symmetrical set of darkwood tables, chairs,

**Above** The Purty Kitchen – once a lodging house for those using the port of Dun Laoghaire

pillars and panels. The ceilings and walls are nicotine-stained and the glass opaque. Some might think it rather glum, but a kinder description would be "fallen grandeur".

Gone are the pewter plates and copper urns. Gone is the Stuart Loving Cup out of which George IV, the merry monarch, supped when he opened Kingstown Harbour here in 1821. Gone is the upstairs cocktail lounge with its panelled Austrian oak in the design of a ship's lounge. Gone is the trellised courtyard that also served as an open-air drinking area.

What remains is a pub with lots of atmosphere, lots of space and no sense of a strain to please. What you see is what you get. The original mahogany counter has been preserved, thankfully, with its six long pump handles, its etched

Dunville whiskey mirror (a now defunct Belfast brand) and its gilt till, which is still operational. Over all these hang wrought-iron lanterns that seem more like chandeliers. A glass-encased pike weighing over 18 pounds has also been preserved, and a cabinet beside it containing various items of silverware. The eponymous kitchen is now a wash-up area for the staff.

Quaint touches include little drawers on the tables and two bare-

**Above** The disarming simplicity of the Purty Kitchen's interior

brick fireplaces, one of which is still used. On the walls are nostalgic advertisements for Player's cigarettes and Will's Cut Golden Bar Tobacco, as well as depictions of Kingstown – now Dun Laoghaire – as it used to be: the Pavilion Harbour, the Town Hall, Lower George's Street and Salthill. The name Kingstown was adopted in King George IV's honour, but was changed to Dun Laoghaire after 1916.

The ferry to Holyhead departs from Dun Laoghaire; it's also popular with tourists for its maritime museum, its yachting centre and its various piers and promenades. The Martello Tower that James Joyce used as the location of the opening chapter of *Ulysses* is also in the vicinity. Joyce lived in the tower for a time and it is now a museum. The Joycean memorabilia includes first editions of his books, a guitar he once owned and his death mask.

**Above** The Purty Kitchen bar with its mahogany counter and partitions

# THE POITÍN STIL

NAAS ROAD, RATHCOOLE

The first thing you notice about this quaint Rathcoole pub is its thatched roof. The name refers to a copper still which is viewable inside. A still, of course, is an apparatus for distilling alcohol. Poitín, or poteen, is the illegal (and potentially lethal) traditional Irish moonshine made from a variety of ingredients including barley, malt and potatoes. There's an old one-liner that goes, "She was only a poteen-maker's daughter, but he loved her still."

The structure dates back to 1643. It was built on what was then Broadmoor common, which was a communal grazing area for cattle, sheep and pigs, and also a place where the locals engaged in social or sporting activities.

There was an inn on the site in 1649 when Oliver Cromwell passed through Rathcoole on his reign of terror. In previous centuries the village showed marked hostility to British attempts at colonisation.

The pub's location has always been a large factor in its success. For over 300 years the main highway to the south of Ireland has stood

**Above** The Poitín Stil has stood for over 300 years on the main highway to the south

nearby. Tolls were collected from coach occupants passing through and they often stopped here overnight, particularly if they had left Dublin in the late afternoon and darkness was falling. Distinguished drinkers who have stopped here include the likes of Jonathan Swift, Charles Stewart Parnell, James Stephens and Daniel O'Connell. It's now just off the Dublin-Naas dual carriageway, attracting today's thirsty travellers. It was originally called the Munster Kings' Inn, but was renamed by current proprietor Louis Fitzgerald when he took it over in 1972. (Fitzgerald has supped the dreaded brew himself in the past and, what's more, lived to tell the tale).

It's divided into many rooms, all of them exuding heady echoes of the past. The Paddock is comprised of stone and sand-blasted pine. Ferkin Corner is an intimate room with an original fireplace and a pitch-pine ceiling. The Stil Room has a roaring turf fire and lots of memorabilia on the walls. This is where the 200-year old still is on view. It's a rather labyrinthine object that looks as if a genie is going to appear out of it in a whiff of smoke. In the Ceoltas Bar you'll hear lashings of trad music. Next door to this is the Hurler's Bar, which is (predictably) frequented by the sporting fraternity. It also attracts the horsey set, as there are a number of racecourses in the vicinity.

**Right** The 200-year-old working spirit still that gives the pub its present name

# JOHNNIE FOX'S

GLENCULLEN, DUBLIN MOUNTAINS

Not only is this the highest pub in Ireland (it's 1000ft above sea level) but also one of the oldest. Built in 1798, the same year as the Wexford Uprising, it has many other connections with nationalist politics beside this coincidental one. Daniel O'Connell used to hold secret meetings here when he lived in Glencullen, and chaired the very first meeting of the Catholic Association here, thus launching the campaign that eventually led to Catholic Emancipation in 1829. In the early 1900s, Michael Collins set up an ammunition factory in one of the outlying buildings of the pub.

Sequestered in a rural hamlet in the middle of the Dublin Mountains, Johnnie Fox's provides an ideal rest spot for backpackers, day-trippers and those of an eco-friendly persuasion. You reach it by turning off the Dublin-Enniskerry Road at Stepaside or Kilternan, and then ascending. And ascending. And ascending. After you've negotiated the climb and the hairpin bends, you'll feel you deserve a treat, and that's exactly what you get.

The place is renowned for its fine seafood cooking, comprising everything from chowder, prawns and mussels to lobster, crab and oysters. Guinness stout heads the list of numerous beers and lagers. There's both whiskey and whisky (a nuance you may care to investigate), an international array of other spirits and a short but decent wine list.

If you're the outdoorsy sort you can walk it all off and survey the panoramic splendour in any number of scenic spots nearby, such as Powerscourt House, a Palladian dwelling set on a 14,000 acre estate.

Highlights include gardens laid out in the Greek and Italian style. There's also a Japanese garden here, and a circular pond with a fountain and statues of winged horses.

The pub is also a haven for traditional music buffs. (Luke Kelly of The Dubliners recorded the original version of "Raglan Road" here in

**Above** Johnnie Fox's is the highest pub in Ireland and one of the oldest

215

the 1960s.) There's entertainment every night in the Parlour Room, featuring ballads, Celtic music, dancing and lots of *craic*. When this place is hopping, it's really hopping.

This isn't one of those opportunistic pubs done up by get-rich-quick publicans: it's the real McCoy. With its blazing logs on the open hearth, its rough stone floor permanently strewn with sawdust and its antique bric-à-brac on the walls, it has changed little with the centuries and is an earthy, unpretentious place. Proprietors Anthony and Geraldine McMahon joke: "We don't let the height of our fame or the fame of our height go to our heads". As you survey its rickety furniture, you're reminded of the American who's alleged to have come in one day and said, "I love your sawdust floors", to which the barman replied, "That's not sawdust; that's last night's furniture!"

The most historic piece of furniture here is a chair that reached some notoriety in 1997. It had been restored for inclusion in an edition of *The Late Late Show*, RTE's longest-running television chat show, and the alleged restorer, one Siubhan Moloney of Donegal, scooped a £1000 award for her troubles. After the show, however, a man called Joshua Duffy claimed that he had done the restoration, not Miss Moloney. She disputed his claim and he sued both her and RTE for defamation of character.

The "Chairgate" saga rolled on for almost three more years, to the bemusement of the Irish populace, before it was finally settled in February 2000. Moloney withdrew her charge, apologised to Duffy and accepted that he had done most of the restoration. She agreed to pay him around £30,000 and there were also legal costs for both parties. It was a large price to pay for £1000 and such brief glory. The irony was that Duffy would have allowed her the glory if she had mentioned him on the show as somebody who helped her. The chair, in any case, became famous as a result.

A sadder incident happened in the pub on New Year's Day 1995, when Elvis Presley impersonator John Reid collapsed after doing a show here. He was resuscitated but it was clear to everyone that he was seriously ill. He died seven days later, on 8 January – Elvis' birthday.

**Previous page and above** Johnnie Fox's is an unpretentious place strewn with bric-a-brac

# THE ROUNDWOOD INN

ROUNDWOOD, WICKLOW

Fans of the Great Outdoors will flock to this former coaching inn. Situated in the heart of the Wicklow hills, far from smog, gridlock and road rage, it affords some breathtaking scenery all around.

One of the biggest draws to the area is spectacular Glendalough (Gaelic for "valley of the two lakes"), a village nestled in the hollow between the surrounding mountains. One of Ireland's most famous monastic sites, it was here that St Kevin, the acclaimed hermit, founded a monastery in the 6th century. It became one of the most vibrant centres of learning in Christendom, attracting pilgrims from all over Britain and the Continent. The holy man is reputed to have lived to the ripe old age of 120, often sleeping in trees or the clefts of rocks.

The best-known story about St Kevin – perhaps apocryphal – relates how he fended off the attentions of a lady called Kathleen with nettles. She was determined to seduce him, the story

**Above** The Roundwood Inn's roaring fires make it a perfect place for tired walkers to relax

goes, so he had to hide from her in a rocky ledge known as St Kevin's Bed. She eventually discovered his hiding-place, which caused him so much distress that he ended up pushing her into the nearest lake. Not very saintly behaviour.

Also in Glendalough is St Kevin's Church, a stone oratory with an 11th century nave and a pitched roof. The church is also somewhat curiously known as St Kevin's Kitchen — possibly because its tower resembles a chimney. The tower acted as a hiding-place for monks when they were being attacked by marauding Vikings. The entrance is high up from the ground. The idea was that they ascended to it by a ladder, which they then pulled up after them, and stayed here until the danger passed. There's also St. Kevin's Cross, an 8th-century celtic structure carved from granite and the 12th-century Priest's House, where those persecuted during Viking raids were buried.

The Roundwood Inn is an elegant pub, boasting polished wooden floors and a crackling log fire (with lanterns on each side) to get you into the romantic mood. The walls are yellow and black. and you drink and/or eat at the sturdy wooden benches. The bar is atmospheric and neat-as-a-new-pin, as one might expect from its German proprietor Jurgen Schwam, who bought it in 1985 and has since put his stamp on everything from the décor to the cuisine — wiener schnitzel and Westphalian ham are the specialities. Flowers and plates sit daintily on the stained wood shelves and there are sketches of an equine theme on the walls.

The public bar is slightly more chummy. Low-ceilinged and also replete with darkwood furniture and an open fire, it's a haven for tired backpackers, an ideal place to wet your whistle and relax in traditional mode.

# INDEX

Abbey Tavern, The 7, 188-191
Abbey Theatre 72, 73, 74, 113
Aherti, Bertie 32, 119, 161
Auld Dubliner, The 9, 140-143
Bailey, The 9, 98-101, 111
Bailey, Nicholas 98
Barnacle, Nora 90
Barry, Margaret 152
Beckett, Samuel 54, 71, 73, 97
Behan, Brendan 48, 77, 90, 93, 97,
101, 102, 104, 107, 110, 126, 136,
155, 156, 157, 162
Bernard, Jeffrey 45
Betjeman, John 136
Bleeding Horse, The 7, 127-129
Bligh, Captain William 174
Bono 144
Boot Inn, The 7, 198-201
Boru, Brian 56, 165
Bowe's 8, 58-59
Bowen, Elizabeth 113
Brady, Paul 119
Brazen Head, The 8, 33, 37, 146, 208
Brereton, William 198
Brian Boru, The 164-167
Brown, Christy 67
Browne, James 71
Bull Island 174, 175
Butt, Isaac 99
Byrne, John Francis 101
Cade, William 77
Carmody, Dermot 53
Casement, Roger 157
Castle Inn, The 8, 25-27
Cat and Cage, The 161-163
Chaplin, Charlie 101
Charles I 149
Charles II 33
Charlton, Jack 32
Childers, Erskine 189
Churchill, Winston 149
Clarence Hotel 9, 144-145
Clarke, Austin 104, 136
Clift, Montgomery 113
Clontarf Castle 170-173
Coachman's Inn, The 7, 202-204
College of Surgeons 108, 131

Collins, Michael 19, 25, 45, 93, 98,
133, 138, 157, 179, 198, 214
Comyn, Archbishop John 26
Connolly, James 68
Conway, Patrick 79
Coughlan, Jim 161
Crist, Gainor 104, 136
Cromwell, Oliver 129, 170, 211
Cronin, Tony 48, 104, 106
Cuchulainn 68
Curran, John Philpott 45
Curran, Sarah 45
Davis, Thomas 54
Davitt, Michael 29
Davy Byrne's 9, 45, 90
Davy, John 130, 132, 133
de Burca, Seamus 77
de Lacy, Hugh 170
de Valera, Éamon 110, 114, 156,
157, 178, 200
Delahunty, John 125
Doheny & Nesbitt's 9, 123-126, 187
Dollymount House 174 175
Donkeavy, JP 10, 19, 90, 92, 100,
104, 129, 136
Dowling, Bridget 114
Drew, Ronnie 32, 118, 119
Drummond, Margaret 178
Dublin Castle 25, 36, 38, 99, 179
Duffy's 7, 192-194
Duke, The 9, 94-97
Edwards, Hilton 77
Elizabeth I 54, 190
Emmet, Robert 36, 45, 54, 108,
200
English, Paddy 155
Faulkner, George 134
Fitzgerald, Lord Edward 22, 24, 25
Fitzmaurice, Thomas 112
Fleming, Niall 125
Flowing Tide, The 8, 72-74
Friel, Brian 73
Fureys, The 119
General Post Office 68, 74, 78
George IV 189, 209, 210
Gildea, Kevin 53
Gill's 155-156

Gilroy, John 13, 186
Glasnevin Cemetery 157-158, 164
Glenside, The 105-107
Gogarty, Oliver St John 54, 100,
113, 120, 138
Goldsmith, Oliver 54
Gregory, Lady Augusta 73
Grogan's 8, 48-50
Griffith, Arthur 93, 98, 157, 200
Guinness, Arthur 11, 12, 13
Hanlon's 152-154
Hartnett, Michael 48
Haughey, Charles 141
Heath Stubbs, John 111
Hedigan, Patrick 164
Hennessy, James 78
Higgins, FR 136
Hitler, Alois 114
Hogan, James 193
Hole in the Wall, The 148-151
Hopkins, Gerard Manley 110, 158
Houlihan, Con 67, 73
Howth Castle 188, 190
Hudson, Rock 113
Huntsman Inn, The 7, 205-207
International, The 8, 51-53
James II 161, 193, 198
Jameson's distillery 11, 13, 139
Johnnie Fox's 7, 214 219
Johnson, Esther 26
Jones, Buck 155
Jordan, John 104
Joyce, James 10, 19, 34, 36, 37, 43,
55, 67, 69, 70, 71, 76, 77, 90, 94,
97, 101, 105, 108, 110, 121, 129,
147, 157, 190, 210
Joyce, James (nationalist rebel)
131, 132
Kavanagh, John 158
Kavanagh, Patrick 48, 94, 101, 102,
104, 107, 110, 121, 136, 162
Kavanagh, Peter 146
Keane, John B 67, 73
Kehoe's 9, 102-103
Kelly, James 154
Kelly, Luke 118, 215
Kennedy, John F 64, 73, 113, 156

# INDEX

Kennedy, Tom 118
Kennelly, Brendan 67
Kettle, Thomas 108
Kipling, Rudyard 113
Kiely, Ben 48, 126
Kilmainham Jail 176, 178, 179
Larkin, James 70
Lavery, Lady 139
Lawlor, William 130
Le Fanu, Sheridan 119, 127, 129
Leinster House 97, 110
Leonard, Hugh 73
Lloyd George, David 93
Long Hall, The 8, 38-41
Long Stone, The 8, 60-62
Lord Edward, The 8, 22-24,
Lord Mayor's, The 7, 195-197
Lynott, Phil 39, 119
Lyons, Alex 53
Mac Thomás, Eamon 36
MacLiammóir, Michael 77
Mael Morda, king of Leinster 164
Malahide Castle 193
Malone, Molly 56
Malone, Timothy 118
Mangan, James Clarence 25
Mansion House 97
Markievicz, Countess 108, 131, 157
Martyn, Edward 73
Masan, James 77
McBride, Maud Gonne 158
McCabe, Christopher 58
McCann, Donal 50, 73
McColl, Ewan 118
McDaid's 9, 48, 102, 104-107,
110, 136
McGuinness, Frank 73
McLoughlin, William 154
McNamara, Brinsley 136
Monks, James 146
Monaghan, Michael 174
Moore, Christy 32, 119
Moore, George 73, 108, 113
Moore, Thomas 24, 54, 200
Morgue 182-184
Morrison, William 170
Mother Red Caps 8, 29-32

Mulligan's 8, 63-67
Murphy, Collin 205
Murphy, Tom 73
Murray, Mrs William 95
Nancy Hand's 8, 80-85
Neary, Leo 111
Neary's 9, 108-111
Nelson, Admiral 69
Newman, John Henry 110
Nixon, John 78
Norseman, The 9, 146-147, 208
Ó Conaire, Pádraic 90
O'Brien, Flann 17, 19, 48, 93, 94,
102, 107, 110, 136
O'Brien, Paddy 48, 100, 106, 107
O'Casey, Sean 62, 74, 139, 161
O'Connell, Daniel 70, 76, 157,
198, 212, 214
O'Donoghue's 9, 116-119
O'Faolain, Sean 113
O'Flaherty, Liam 48, 104
O'Hanlon, Ardal 53
O'Malley, Queen Grace 190
O'Neill's 8, 54-57
O'Shea, Kitty 76, 99, 157
O'Shea, Captain William 76
O'Toole, Peter 110, 113
Old Stand, The 8, 45-47
Oliver St John Gogarty, The
9, 138-139
Oval, The 8, 68-71
Palace, The 9, 134-137
Parnell, Charles Stewart 19, 29, 75,
99, 157, 212
Parnell Mooney 8, 75, 77
Patrick Conway's 8, 75, 78-79
Patriots Inn, The 176-179
Pearse, Patrick 68, 78, 110
Penny Black, The 180-181
Petty, Sir William 10
Plunkett, Joseph Mary 178
Poitín Stil, The 7, 211-213
Portobello, The 9, 130-133
Power's distillerery 11, 13, 14, 53
Powerscourt, Viscount 50
Purcell, Noel 104
Purty Kitchen, The 7, 208-210

Quigley, Martin S 114
Reedy, Christopher 118
Reid, John 219
Reynolds, Thomas 36
Rich, Barnaby 10
Roundwood Inn, The 7, 220-222
Royal Kilmainham Hospital 176, 179
Ryan, John 99, 101, 105, 111,
135, 136
Ryan, Thomas J. 45
Ryan's of Parkgate 9, 86-89
St James' Gate Brewery 11, 13
St Kevin 220, 222
St Patrick's Cathedral 26
St Stephen's Green 108, 131, 132
Scott-Lennon, James 191
Shaw Weaver, Harriet 94
Shelbourne Hotel 9, 112-115
Sitric, Viking king 164, 191
Smith, Tommy 48, 50
Smyllie, Robert 135, 136, 137
Smyth's 168-169
Stag's Head, The 8, 42-44
Stephens, James 212
Stone Boat 187
Stoker, Bram 54, 129
Strevell, John 38
Swift, Jonathan 26, 212
Synge, John Millington 19, 54, 74
Talbot, Richard 193
Temple, Sir William 141
Thackeray, William 113
Tickerell, Thomas 165
Tone, Wolfe 19, 54, 108
Toner's 9, 16, 120-122
Tristram, Almeric 188
Turner, Martyn 115
Turner, Richard 165
Trinity College 54, 55, 62, 141
Vaughn, George 118
Walsh, Dick 125
Ward, John 176
Waugh, Evelyn 101
Wilde, William 119
William III 161, 193, 198
Woods, Macdara 48
Yeats, WB 73, 74, 94, 105, 119, 120